W9-CCS-179

DISCARD

A PORTRAIT OF THE ARTIST AS A YOUNG MAN

Voices of the Text

TWAYNE'S MASTERWORK STUDIES
ROBERT LECKER, GENERAL EDITOR

A PORTRAIT OF THE ARTIST AS A YOUNG MAN

Voices of the Text

MARGUERITE HARKNESS

Twayne Publishers • *Boston*

A DIVISION OF G. K. HALL & CO.

A Portrait of the Artist as a Young Man: Voices of the Text
Marguerite Harkness

Twayne's Masterwork Studies No. 38
Copyright 1990 by G. K. Hall & Co.
All rights reserved.
Published by Twayne Publishers
A division of G. K. Hall & Co.
70 Lincoln Street, Boston, Massachusetts

Copyediting supervised by Barbara Sutton.
Book production by Gabrielle B. McDonald.

Typeset in 10/14 Sabon by Compset, Inc. of Beverly, Massachusetts

Printed on permanent/durable acid-free paper
and bound in the United States of America.

Library of Congress Cataloging-in-Publication Data

Harkness, Marguerite.
    A portrait of the artist as a young man : voices of the text / Marguerite Harkness.
        p.   cm.—(Twayne's masterwork studies ; no. 38)
    Includes bibliographical references.
    Includes Index.
    ISBN 0-8057-8064-5 (alk. paper).—ISBN 0-8057-8125-0 (pbk. : alk. paper)
    1. Joyce, James, 1882–1941.   Portrait of the artist as a young man.
    I. Title.   II. Series.
PR6019.09P6447   1990
823'.912—dc20   89-36945
                                                                                CIP

For the carpenter critic

CONTENTS

NOTE ON THE REFERENCES
AND ACKNOWLEDGMENTS

All references to James Joyce's *A Portrait of the Artist as a Young Man* are to the Viking Critical Edition, edited by Chester Anderson and Richard Ellmann (New York: Viking, 1968).

I wish to acknowledge the kind permission to quote from *A Portrait of the Artist as a Young Man* by James Joyce. Copyright 1916 by B. W. Huebsch, renewed 1944 by Nora Joyce. © 1964 by the Estate of James Joyce. Reprinted by permission of Viking Penguin Inc., Jonathan Cape, Ltd., and the Society of Authors as the literary representative of the Estate of James Joyce.

This book has one name on the title page, but others have contributed mightily to it. Teachers and students, colleagues and friends have tolerated or enjoyed my obsession with Joyce's novel for years now, and their readings and responses have taught me much—intellectual and emotional debts that cannot be acknowledged in footnotes. I can only wish all readers the good fortune of such comrades in reading.

I have incurred some debts of a more specific kind as I wrote this book. The Sterling Library and the Joyce Centre at the University of London permitted me to use their collections during a summer in England, and I thank them for their courtesy. More crucially, Boyd Berry, Sally Doud, Dorothy Fillmore, and Richard Priebe—friends and colleagues at Virginia Commonwealth University—read parts or all of the manuscript at various stages of my writing, saving me more than one embarrassment and cheering me on. (Errors, misjudgments, blind spots remain my own.) I can only wish all writers the good fortune of such comrades in writing.

JAMES JOYCE (1882–1941)
Photograph courtesy of the Beinecke Rare Book and Manuscript Library, Yale University.

CHRONOLOGY:
JAMES JOYCE'S LIFE AND WORKS

1882	James Augustine Joyce born 2 February to John Stanislaus Joyce and Mary Jane Murray Joyce, their first son, in Rathgar, a fashionable suburb of Dublin, Ireland.
1887	Joyces move to 1 Martello Terrace in Bray, a resort-like suburb south of Dublin, where they entertain and house "Dante" Hearn Conway and John Kelly of Tralee (the models for Dante and Mr. Casey in *Portrait*). The Vances with their daughter Eileen live at 4 Martello Terrace.
1888	Attends Clongowes Wood College, a boarding school run by the Jesuits.
1889–1890	Period of Charles Stewart Parnell's political problems. Ultimately Parnell's political party ousts him from power after he is named as corespondent in a divorce suit.
1891	Leaves Clongowes Wood College; his father, who has lost his job as collector of rates, fails to make the last tuition payment.
1891	Parnell dies 6 October. Joyce writes *Et Tu, Healy!* on the betrayal and death of Parnell.
1891	After a violent fight on Christmas Day, Dante Conway leaves the Joyce home within five days.
1892	The Joyce family begins repeated moves to less and less fashionable quarters as they slide into poverty.
1893	Enrolls as a scholarship student at Belvedere, an exclusive Jesuit school.
1894	John Stanislaus Joyce liquidates the last of his holdings in Cork. James wins the first of several exam prizes.
1895	Joins the Sodality of the Blessed Virgin Mary.
1896	Father James A. Cullen comes to Belvedere on 30 November to conduct a retreat based closely on Loyola's *Spiritual Exercises*.

1897–1898   Begins *Silhouettes*, short fiction in a decidedly realistic mode, according to Stanislaus—none survives. Begins also *Moods*, his first collection of poetry: only a fragment survives. Period of national revival in Ireland: the Gaelic League, the Gaelic Athletic League, the Irish National Literary Society active in Dublin. The dean of studies suggests that Joyce may have a vocation; Joyce rejects the idea. In September 1898 enters University College, Dublin.

1900   Writes a review of Ibsen's *When We Dead Awaken* for the *Fortnightly Review;* published 1 April.

1901   Publishes "The Day of the Rabblement."

1902   Publishes "James Clarence Mangan"; graduates from UCD; leaves for Paris.

1903   Publishes twenty-one reviews. April, his mother dying, sees Joyce return to Dublin for her death and funeral. She dies in August.

1904   Writes "A Portrait of the Artist." Writes and publishes poems and four stories in the *Irish Homestead*. Lives in the Martello tower with Oliver St. John Gogarty. Meets Nora Barnacle and leaves Dublin, essentially for good.

1904–1913   Lives and teaches in Trieste, Paris, and Rome. Giorgio, Joyce's son, born 1905. Writes the stories of *Dubliners*, which is accepted for publication by Grant Richards in 1906. Richards, and later a Dublin firm, refuse to publish for fear of obscenity and/or libel actions. Joyce's daughter, Lucia, born 1906.

1913   Ezra Pound, prompted by Yeats, contacts Joyce; Richards reconsiders *Dubliners*.

1914   Publishes *Dubliners*. Joyce is writing *A Portrait of the Artist as a Young Man* and *Exiles*. Serial publication of *Portrait* in *The Egoist* begins, with the assistance of Ezra Pound.

1915   Begins *Ulysses*. Italy's entry into World War I forces Joyce and his family to flee Trieste and find refuge in Zurich where they spend the war years. Receives grant from the English Royal Literary Fund.

1916   Publishes *Portrait*.

1917   First of many eye operations occurs.

1918   *Little Review* begins serial publication of *Ulysses*, but halts under obscenity codes. With the end of World War I, the Joyces return to Trieste.

1920   Moves to Paris where he lives until the outbreak of World War II again threatens him with internment as a British citizen.

Chronology: James Joyce's Life and Work

1922	After various difficulties, again from fears of libel or obscenity charges, Sylvia Beach publishes the first edition of *Ulysses* in Paris. The first copy comes to Joyce on his birthday, 2 February.
1923	Begins *Finnegans Wake.*
1931	Joyce and Nora marry, largely to protect his estate and guarantee the legitimacy of his children. Joyce is writing *Finnegans Wake*, which, like his other works, is published serially.
1933	*Ulysses,* in a landmark court case, is admitted to the United States; the obscenity charge is overruled.
1939	Publishes *Finnegans Wake.*
1939	World War II begins. Joyce is in France with a draft-aged son, a daughter in a mental hospital, and a British passport.
1940	Attempts to find ways to move his whole family from Paris to Zurich, fighting the illness that will eventually kill him. He, Nora, Giorgio, Stephen (Giorgio's son) arrive in Zurich.
1941	Dies in Zurich and is buried there.

Chapter 1

HISTORICAL CONTEXT

In the first three months of 1882, the year of James Joyce's birth, the Royal Irish Constabulary reported 1,417 "agrarian outrages"—attacks upon landowners and their property—in what has been labeled Ireland's Land War.[1] In April 1916, two months after the first publication of *A Portrait of the Artist as a Young Man* in book form, a small band of Irish republicans, standing on the balcony of the General Post Office, declared a republic; the British army and constabulary put down the revolt, executed the leaders, and returned its energies to its major war in France. The young James Joyce, and the period in which he came to maturity, witnessed serial waves of nationalist agitation, for the central fact of Irish history during the period was that Ireland was a poor, underdeveloped colony of England, despite its official status as a member, not a colony, of Great Britain, the Union of Wales, Scotland, Ireland, and England. The Irish did not perceive themselves as an equal partner in the federation, and indeed they were not.

If we compare Ireland's condition with England's, we discover massive inequities. The British government labeled over half of the population of Dublin unskilled and unemployed[2]; the sanitary conditions of Dublin ranked far behind any in the cities of England; the infant mortality rate "for children of labourers" was 27.7 per 1,000 in 1905; "the death-rate in Dublin in 1911 [was] . . . 27.6 per 1,000 . . . higher than any other city in Europe"; and housing conditions in Dublin suggest that most laboring families lived in a room and a half.[3] Compare that to the number of rooms indicated in mining villages in D. H. Lawrence's novels, where clearly the houses had kitchens, front parlors, and more than one bedroom. Historian Edward Norman proposes that these kinds of comparisons evade the issue: to compare Ireland with England is to compare an agrarian, peasant economy with an industrial one.[4] For him, the more apt comparison would, presumably, be with Britain's colonies in Africa or Asia. The catch is, and for Irish nationalists it was a catch, that Ireland was not officially a colony but a member of the Union after 1801. By 1896, English parliamentary reports demonstrated that Ireland had been unfairly taxed (that is, it had not paid taxes as a peasant economy but as an industrial economy) for decades. From 1896 to 1914, the English response was to pour enormous funds into Ireland, in attempts both to remedy inequities[5] and, less charitably, to lessen the numbers and severity of the "agrarian outrages" that the Irish peasant engaged in and to discourage those who wished political separation. Despite such amelioration of Ireland's condition, nationalists were not content.

Under England's colonial rule, Irish land had been transferred from the indigenous Gaels to Englishmen or transplanted Scots. These imported landowners and their descendants came to be known as the "Anglo-Irish Ascendancy," marking both their ambiguous nationality (Anglo-Irish) and their socal class (ascendant). By 1770, Roman Catholics (and almost all the original Gaels were Catholics rather than Protestants) owned only one-twentieth of the land of their forefathers.[6] Although many nationalists of the nineteenth century—including Charles Stewart Parnell and William Butler Yeats—belonged to the Ascendancy, for some Irish nationalists, its mere existence was the historical proof of England's exploitation of their country. Land ownership or management figured centrally in the Irish political agitation of the nineteenth century, culminating in the Wyndham Act of 1903, whereby most Irish tenants could buy the land they worked with low-cost loans from the British government. But in the year of Joyce's birth, that solution was only hinted at in the Land Act of 1881, the first effort to provide the means for Gaelic Irish to buy land.

To understand how crucial land ownership was we can profitably look back to the first half of the century. Most of the Irish were rural land tenants, paying rent either to a slightly more prosperous farmer or directly to the landlords. Historian Joel Mokyr claims that there were only about 8,000 landowners in 1841; 62 percent of the Irish were "laborers, smallholders, and other persons 'without capital, in either money, land, or acquired knowledge.'"[7] The per-capita income of the Irish in 1841 was £15.22 while England's per-capita income was £24.43.[8] Small farms and almost total dependence upon the potato crop made the potato blight of the forties disastrous. In 1847, at the height of the famine, England ceased famine relief. Mokyr argues convincingly that English prejudice against the Irish caused that decision: the British treasury had enough money a few years later to spend "£ 69.3 Million on an utterly futile adventure in the Crimea."[9] Whatever the famine's actual death toll—and most seem to think it around a million and a half—the English failure to continue poor relief exacerbated Irish antipathy and encouraged increased agitation over land-ownership, tenants' rights, and fair rents.

That agitation found its focus in the Irish Land League, formed officially by Michael Davitt and Charles Stewart Parnell. Months before its official founding, the Irish smallholder faced another possible potato famine. In the summer of 1879, "the potato blight suddenly returned with disastrous virulence, destroying the entire crop in Connaught and creating all the natural conditions of 1847"; Parnell urged farmers, just before the blight hit, "'You must show them [the landlords] that you intend to hold a firm grip of your homesteads and lands. You must not allow yourselves to be dispossessed as your fathers were dispossessed in 1847.'"[10] The Land War began. In 1880, Parnell called for shunning—later called boycotting—of predatory landlords and those who took leases on land from which others had been evicted. The Land League was held responsible, at least in part, for the agrarian outrages of the early 1880s. Rural agitation, much more than any proletarian urban revolt, forced British governments to compromise with Irish parliamentary leader Parnell. Less politically radical than many nationalists (he wanted constitutional change that would preserve the Union), Parnell repeatedly forced concessions by one English administration only to have them withdrawn by another or the same administration when circumstances changed.

By 1881, Parnell was the recognised leader of the nationalist movement. When he was named corespondent in a divorce suit in 1891 (an event that figures prominently in *Portrait*), first the British prime minister (Gladstone), then the political rivals Parnell had outmaneuvered earlier, then the Roman Catholic church denounced him as unfit to lead. His political party was split over the issue. Unfortunately for Irish nationalists, Parnell's success in amassing personal political control meant that there was no one with sufficient political power to lead, and the effective coalition between constitutionalists, would-be revolutionaries, and the Irish peasantry collapsed. At the same time, a conservative British government with an overwhelming majority in the Houses of Parliament guaranteed that the issue of Home Rule for Ireland was dead by 1895.[11]

In this context, it is perhaps amazing or perhaps predictable that Ireland produced writers of such brilliance. Relative to its population, Ireland produced a disproportionate number of celebrated and critically acclaimed writers: Wilde, Shaw, Yeats, Synge, O'Casey, Joyce. If it was not a prosperous time to be Irish, it was, apparently, a fortuitous time for Irish writing. Inevitably, almost no Irish writer could write without reference to his or her benighted country.

If we look beyond Ireland, we can see that nationalist sympathies were widespread in Europe during the same period leading up to World War I. It is possible to read some of the Irish context as simply an exacerbated version of European nationalism. With all of these nationalistic movements, there were cultural as well as political and economic aspects. So the collecting of national folklore in Germany has a parallel in the efforts of the Irish to recover an indigenous culture.

Yeats, Douglas Hyde, and Lady Gregory engaged in such cultural nationalism, even when they distrusted the political and revolutionary nationalism around them. The Irish Literary Movement and later the Irish National Theatre are manifestations of that kind of nationalism. Joyce knew these groups too, and while he did not join in their members' efforts, neither did he join their detractors, refusing to sign petitions protesting the Irish theater's portrayal of the Irish.

The turn of the century witnessed enormous changes in literary practices, too. Widespread literacy and the technology to mass produce books increased the demand for accessible, less demanding stories, poems, and essays. Literary production increasingly divided into mass-produced, popular works and small-press, "beautiful" books.[12] Literary artists chose their side and most of those we call "classical modernists" chose Milton's "fit audience though few." Joyce was no exception. While he may have wished to capture all readers, the surface difficulties, the daring realism, and the precision of his writing placed him with other high modernists like Yeats, Eliot, and Pound. Certainly after *Portrait*, his works were only accessible to attentive and patient readers.

At the same time, writers were faced with two competing notions about art. On the one hand, writers like Émile Zola and Thomas Hardy produced naturalist fiction. Responding to the work of scientists and social scientists, especially in England to Herbert Spenser's *The Study of Sociology*,[13] they depicted human life realistically; at times, they saw human beings as creatures at the mercy of their environment and biology. The title of Zola's theoretical treatise, *The Experimental Novel*,[14] reflects the influence of science on letters. On the other hand, Arthur Rimbaud, Charles Baudelaire, and Stéphane Mallarmé in France and Arthur Symons, Oscar Wilde, William Morris, and Yeats in Great Britain practiced the more magical, less scientific art we call "symbolism." Symons's *The Symbolist Movement in Literature*[15] (dedicated to Yeats) publicized for English readers the French innovations. One task of any twentieth-century writer was to choose or to select from among these notions about art and to carve out his own practice.

Joyce's work clearly shows that he attempted to fuse these two traditions. Stephen Dedalus's portrait shows him both as a product of his environment (and hence determined) and as a character drawn to the magical nature of art. Stephen claims in the last chapter that the soul of man is imprisoned in Ireland by "nationality, language, religion," what he calls "nets" that hold the soul from flight.[16] These are cultural nets, nets perpetuated by environment, while Stephen's escape, in his view, will occur through art, a timeless, placeless, magical gift. His choice to be "a priest of eternal imagination, transmuting the daily bread of experience into the radiant body of everliving life" (221) clearly aligns him with the *symbolistes*. Transmuting that "daily bread" requires, in his view, transcending the daily round of life, finding in art a better and purer life; Stephen believes that he can escape environment. Yet Joyce's depiction of his character demonstrates that environment does, at least in part, determine character, and that even Stephen's decisions to transcend Dublin and to turn to symbolist art are environmentally conditioned.

In short, the literary debate between naturalists and symbolists, occurring just prior to and during Joyce's youth and maturity, itself raised questions about how fully Irish poverty and nationalism formed a character and how such a character might "transcend" his culture. Because Joyce pursued such questions in his writing, it is essential to know the economic, social, and political contexts as well as the literary debates in England and on the Continent: those literary debates form part of the environment that shapes self-expression and, if one is lucky, may provide a satisfactory "mode of life or art" (247) for it. Many of the obstacles Stephen encounters are the products of his environment; they manifest Joyce's naturalistic world view. While Stephen sees in symbolism the means to surmount those naturalistic obstacles, Joyce demonstrates that even the means of escape is environmentally produced: the literary environment made symbolism available to Stephen as a means of self-expression and escape. Ultimately, perhaps Joyce himself surmounted obstacles in his life through his own realistic and symbolic art.

Chapter 2

THE IMPORTANCE OF
THE WORK

Samuel Johnson said a classic was a work that pleased many and pleased long. I would add "intrigued many and intrigued long." Novels that reward each reading with a new sense of themselves, a new sense of ourselves, and a new sense of mystery are classics. For me, and for many other readers, *A Portrait of the Artist as a Young Man* is such a novel.

For many first-time readers, their own age affects the story they read. To read this novel as a young adult or adolescent is to find, "mirrored perfectly in a lucid supple periodic prose" (167), one's own frustrations with the world. Authorities threaten to destroy youth and freedom as they attempt to mold us into properly socialized adults whose thoughts and spirits contribute unthinkingly to the status quo. That is not because adults are vicious, but because, inherently, they protect what they are and the culture that made them so. Even adults whose culture has denied them success and satisfaction enforce on their children some rules of that culture. Finding a young rebel who opposes those codes that threaten his freedom, or one whose experience with religion mirrors the experiences of many adolescents, or one who is intelligent and misunderstood, appeals to anyone who has experienced rebellion at a similar age. The young, and young males in particular, identify with the protagonist. No matter how jaded, sophisticated, mature, or cynical readers become, this first response to the trials and growth of Stephen Dedalus remains. It remains for the young Seventh Day Adventist who swears that he, too, has heard the sermons on hell that Stephen hears, that he too has felt the overwhelming power of the Church trying to dominate his life, that he too has found a way—however unpleasant it has been for his churchgoing parents—of escaping that world, at least for a time. It remains for all of us who have heard since childhood various voices telling us what to do with our lives.

Reading the novel later has different rewards. Some may identify their younger selves with Stephen Dedalus while they detach their mature selves from the callowness of his youth. They may find that they have escaped Stephen's overzealous pride, or have outgrown it. They may, as some critics in the fifties did, come to hate Stephen; to me, that hatred is of tendencies we fear in ourselves, tendencies toward solipsism, arrogance, indifference to the emotions of others. We tend to hate what threatens us, and this hatred may depend on simultaneous identification with this creature of Joyce.

Those who read the novel in academic settings or for pleasure find yet different rewards, which are in many ways simply more sophisticated versions of the childhood rewards of rhyme, of made up words, of rap music, of elegance in slang: the play of language and words. For the novel is filled with that play. The novel, written with such care that Joyce's word *scrupulous* seems appropriate,[1] offers the joy of making and seeing pattern among words and emotional associations. The words *cold* and *hot* become suggestive, evocative descriptions, for instance, tracing Stephen's response to his environment, to his religion, to art, to life. The joy a mathematician or scientist experiences when the most elegant solution occurs to him or her parallels the joy a reader can experience in precise, polished, elegant prose where each word does, indeed, seem to count, where superfluities seem nonexistent. It is a well-made novel by a master craftsman.

Others read this novel because it allows them to enter a world they do not live in. Imaginative sympathy allows us to participate in such a world if it is finely enough drawn, detailed enough to come to life for us. To get a sense of the political intrigues of Dublin, of the nationalist views of the English–Irish conflict, of the enormous power of the Roman Catholic church in the lives of ordinary Irish people as Joyce constructs them in his novel intrigues and rewards those of us who are curious about others and their lives.

All of those responses are valid and are perhaps the reason this novel lives in our literature. At the same time, the position assigned to this novel by literary history is owed to its experimental nature, its newness, its modernity. In the history of our literature, this novel stands out as a new beginning, a new way of writing novels. The experiments initiated by Joyce in *Portrait* affect and reflect the map of twentieth-century novels; he, like others of the century, found in prose a way to write poetry; he, like others of the century, enacted a philosophical and scientific "discovery": that truth resides only within the individual and within the perceptions we choose to call shared; it is not external to human shaping and control. Nothing is "real" outside the human imagination. The novel insists upon this view and is one of the early dramatic statements of that reality. Stephen's character is communicated by the ways in which he shapes and helps create the reality he sees, as Joyce explored how we create our own realities.

That exploration depended upon words to mirror the process of creation as well as what the internal self creates. While Yeats had already written "words alone are certain good,"[2] Joyce acts out the corollary: words alone exist, and only through words do we construct and communicate reality. Although Joyce's experiments with form and the "new" words he coins are less obvious in *Portrait* than in his later works, the etymologies of words, slang, and sound in *Portrait* nevertheless establish the reality that the narrative constructs—the reality that contains and conveys and *is* Stephen Dedalus and his experiences.

Portrait was the first novel by the man who would eventually write two of the first truly experimental novels of the twentieth century: *Ulysses* and *Finnegans Wake*. In that role, *Portrait* prepares us to read startlingly experimental fiction that, through happenstance and skill, and unlike many literary experiments of the twentieth century, has survived to be read fifty years after its composition. Their survival rate may be due, as much as anything, to the very ordinary topics or obsessions of James Joyce: the family, adolescent yearnings for division and escape, the love of men and women.

And that point brings me back to my first: novels that seem to enact a human drama please and intrigue many, and please and intrigue long. *A Portrait of the Artist as a Young Man* is one of those novels.

Chapter 3

CRITICAL RECEPTION

Readers today may find the publishing history and initial reception of *A Portrait of the Artist as a Young Man* bizarre. Having written the novel, Joyce submitted it to a series of publishers, the last being Duckworth. There the reader, Edward Garnett, reported that the "public will call the book . . . realistic, unprepossessing, unattractive," despite the fact that he thought it "ably written." The novel was, in his view, unnecessarily ugly; the diary section at the end was a "complete falling to bits" of the novel; it would have to be entirely rewritten.[1] On 18 May 1915 Duckworth rejected the novel. Whatever we think of the novel at a distance of seventy plus years, Garnett was prescient about the initial responses of negative critics: some found it ugly; one found the diary evidence of the hero's insanity. The Duckworth reader did not foresee, however, other readers who hailed the novel as a major event in English literature, a new and realistic novel.

Portrait was first published serially in the *Egoist* thanks to Ezra Pound's intervention and interest in Joyce's prose. From 2 February 1914 to September 1915, sections of the novel appeared to some intense reaction. In 1916, after Duckworth's rejection, Harriet Weaver (editor of the *Egoist*) agreed to publish it in book form. Several printers refused to set the type; according to Richard Ellmann, they were frightened by the recent censorship of D. H. Lawrence's *The Rainbow*.[2] (One of the peculiarities of English libel and obscenity laws was that typesetters were personally libel.) Finally in October 1916, B. W. Huebsch agreed to publish the novel in New York; it appeared 29 December 1916.

While boosters like Ezra Pound continued to call *Portrait* a novel of genius, many reviewers were less sympathetic. Almost unanimously, reviewers recognized that Joyce's novel was realistic, although they disagreed about whether such a quality was positive. So, for instance, one negative reviewer ended by announcing, "The tradition in English fiction . . . is not in the direction of Russian realism [an association that runs through many early reviews], and we cannot say that we regret it"[3]; another in *Freeman's Journal* complained that Joyce "drags his readers after him into the slime of foul sewers"[4]; and yet another claimed that no "clear-thinking man" would let "his wife, his sons or daughters" come near the book—despite its realism.[5] Even John Quinn, a vociferous supporter of Joyce's works, thought it "perhaps not a book for all young women," though "no young man or young woman of the right fibre would be harmed by it."[6] In *Everyman,* a baffled but not entirely negative reviewer reported it as an "astonishingly powerful and extraordinary dirty study of the upbringing of a young man by Jesuits, which ends—so far as we have been at all able to unravel the meaning of the impressionistic ending—with his insanity."[7]

For most of these reviewers, Joyce seemed too concerned with the dunghill and its smell (it is amazing how many comment on the obnoxious odors of Stephen's world); even essentially positive reviewers—H. G. Wells, A. Clutton-Brock, reviewers in the *Manchester Guardian* and the *New Statesman*—remarked on this aspect, the last claiming that "Joyce can never resist a dunghill."[8]

Despite such reservations or outright rejections of the novel, Joyce received extraordinary praise as well. Reviewers recognized that the "technique" was "startling," in H. G. Wells's words.[9] More than one remarked on Joyce's ability to capture conversation: "as close to the dialogue of life as anything I have ever come across."[10] A. Clutton-Brock proclaimed, "No living author is better at conversations."[11]

Reviewers seemed to be speaking of the same novel, regardless of their judgments about it, when they turned to the style and plot. In *Literary World,* a negative review claimed it was a "study of a temperament [rather] than a story in the ordinary sense."[12] In a positive review, the *New Republic* reported that all readers "will see at once that [Joyce] has never even thought of a 'plot' in the ordinary sense." The narrative, according to this reviewer, "requires some imagination" from the reader.[13] The *New Statesman* echoed: "There is no 'plot.'"[14] At the same time, the positive reviewers saw that the plotlessness of the novel contributed significantly to the massive realism Joyce achieved. Here is just one such review: "Episodes, sensations, dreams, emotions trivial or tragic succeed each other neither coherently nor incoherently; each is developed vividly for a moment, then fades away into the next, with or without the mechanical devices of chapter division or rows of stars. *Life is so . . . .*"[15] In this "fundamentally true" novel (John F. Harris in *To-Day*),[16] the naked realism, the extraordinary attempt to capture what Virginia Woolf called, "the flickerings of that innermost flame which flashes its myriad messages through the brain,"[17] garnered from its adherents the highest praise.

If the first twenty-five years of *Portrait*'s history was spent judging it, the last forty-five have been spent explaining it. While the initial reception may have been too focused on determining its value or lack of it, we might wonder if critical judgment has entirely disappeared to be replaced by praise-songs. Almost all current commentary upon the novel assumes it to be a classic and worthy of any amount of explanation. It is perhaps fair to say that Joycean scholarship as we know it began with Harry Levin's *James Joyce: A Critical Introduction* in 1941,[18] coincidentally the year of Joyce's death, and Irene Hendry Chayes's pioneering work on Joyce's epiphanies[19]; both studies not only opened the doors for the prolonged and accelerating study of the novel, but continue to be useful to all readers. Chayes's essay, in particular, informs (at least tacitly all discussions of *Portrait* in the last forty years.

For more recent critics, issues of realism and style remain central to the conversation. We can see broad outlines of approaches and attitudes about this novel over the last forty years. For decades, most critics regarded the novel at least in part as Joyce's view of himself, his confession to the world of his artistry and his superiority to the reader. By 1950, in part under the influence of what we once called the New Critics, persons began not to identify Stephen with Joyce, but to see irony in Joyce's treatment of his protagonist. Questions of authorial attitude inevitably lead critics into discussions of narrative point of view, of the attitude of the author toward his character and the events of the novel.

In 1955, Hugh Kenner proposed quite ferociously (a position he later modified) such a distance between Joyce and Stephen that the conversations among critics appeared to be divided into those who "hated" Stephen and those who found him the epitome of the proper artist, the image of Joyce the creator.[20] Wayne Booth in *The Rhetoric of Fiction* proposed that we cannot determine Joyce's relationship to Stephen because the novel is flawed.[21] Robert Scholes, on the other hand, argued both that the novel tells us all we need to know and that Stephen is a successful poet at the end, having struggled through his own gestation.[22]

The fights engendered by Kenner's blast against Stephen gradually dwindled, for most readers of Joyce will agree that Joyce's irony is mixed, uneven, alloyed with identification. Nonetheless, for readers today—whether practicing critics or not—the questions of how Joyce regards his protagonist and whether Stephen is successful in his rebellion against the forces of his childhood remain. How we are to take or understand this novel depends, as in all novels, on how we understand its conclusion, a conclusion that puzzled early reviewers as well. That issue is still open to debate. Some of the most recent criticism argues that the questions cannot be resolved, that the glory of the novel depends upon their insolubility, at least in part, because reality contains unanswerable questions, insoluble problems.

In 1952, Richard Kain and Marvin Magalaner's *Joyce: The Man, the Work, the Reputation*[23] brought together current attitudes and concerns about Joyce's works. Surveying the difficulties of Joyce criticism, they concluded that "Joyce's biography is very much a problem—in fact, *the* problem of Joyce scholarship,"[24] for the authorized biography by Herbert Gorman[25] was immediately recognized as biased, nonscholarly, too little revelatory of Joyce the man and the writer. By the late fifties, the Joyce industry not only had a biography it wished to call its own—Richard Ellmann's eight hundred page *James Joyce*[26]—but a warming up of a critical and scholarly factory dedicated to finding the "facts." In one area of Joyce's life, his religious training and background, the interest in knowing about him spawned two books,[27] but also studies of how he used his Catholicism (particularly helpful was Father Noon's *Joyce and Aquinas*[28]). Like archaeologists, Joyceans poured over city maps to locate every cobblestone (and firm and street and church, of course) mentioned in the works of Joyce. They researched the writers he might have read, rejected or ignored; they counted and identified song references; they sought—and found—the model on which Joyce drew for the hell sermons preached in chapter 3 of *Portrait;* they investigated his childhood for traces of Freudian difficulties; they inquired into the relationships between James Joyce and his friends.

His friends published memoirs: John Francis Byrne (the model for Cranly in *Portrait*) bought out *Silent Years: An Autobiography with Memoirs of James Joyce and Our Ireland*[29]; Mary and Padraic Colum (both Irish writers of some note), *Our Friend James Joyce*[30]; Leon Edel, *James Joyce: The Last Journey*[31]; Constantine Curran, *James Joyce Remembered.*[32] These works revealed the obvious parallels between the fictional life of Stephen Dedalus and the life that Ellmann and others detail for James Joyce. Other investigations proceeded: the first version of the novel, an essay with the title, "A Portrait of an Artist" was sold to Cornell University by Stanislaus Joyce and published in 1960 in the *Yale Review;* Robert Scholes and Richard Kain collected various background materials into *The Workshop of Daedalus: James Joyce and the Raw Materials for "A Portrait of the Artist as a Young Man,"*[33] including the early draft, short prose epiphanies from Joyce's notebooks, his writings on aesthetics, and excerpts from other writers that inform Joyce's novel. Joseph Prescott explored the relationship between the second version of Joyce's autobiographical novel, *Stephen Hero* (1944) and *Portrait*.[34]

Concurrent with these efforts to establish the "reality" of Joyce's story were repeated efforts to trace motif, symbol, and image through the novel. So, for instance, William York Tindall's *A Reader's Guide to James Joyce*[35] emphasized the symbolic and imagistic unity of *Portrait*. The experience of reading the novel, as Kain and Magalaner suggest, leads critics in two directions, for the surface of the novel—with its place names and dates—encourages naturalistic investigation, while its apparent (though not actual) "plotlessness" impels readers to study "the expressive reiteration of an action, a situation, or a speech."[36]

By the sixties, *Portrait* was so firmly established as canonical literature that three volumes of collected essays appeared in the space of six years.[37] These collections were largely reprints of influential essays on the novel—essays that general readers might have difficulty assembling. Such collections mark the arrival of Joyce's novel in academia and the increased activity of the Joyce industry in promulgating itself.

The sixties, too, saw repeated excursions into Joyce's aesthetic theory—in *Stephen Hero*, in his Paris notebooks, in *Portrait* itself, and, of course, in the later works. Indeed, Connolly devotes 120 pages of his 330-page collection to discussions of aesthetics; while Nault and Morris devote seventy. In 1962, the same year Connolly and Nault and Morris published, Ryf brought out *A New Approach to Joyce: "A Portrait of the Artist" as Guidebook*,[38] which proposes Joyce's first novel as the script for his later work.

As critics learned more and more about Joyce's biography and recovered and reproduced early versions of his novel, several critics focused on the development of Joyce's art. In 1959, Marvin Magalaner's *Time of Apprenticeship*[39] appeared; in 1972, Homer Obed Brown's *James Joyce's Early Fiction*[40] focused more intently upon the movement from the last story in *Dubliners* ("The Dead") to *Portrait*, especially as both those works seem to reveal a Joyce more sympathetic to his characters and less vitriolic about the failings of the Irish.

Critical Reception

In 1976, fifty years after *Portrait*'s publication, in a collection to celebrate its birth, Hans Walter Gabler took critics back to the beginning, detailing what the manuscript evidence can tell us about how James Joyce wrote this novel. In a wonderfully instructive essay, Gabler shows the true colors of a scholar detective.[41]

Analyses of Joyce's novel have followed trends in contemporary criticism: psychological critics, poststructuralists, feminists, marxists have all been moved to comment on *Portrait*. Studies of psychological theory as applied to Joyce began appearing with regularity in the early 1970s: Edmund Epstein's *The Ordeal of Stephen Dedalus;*[42] Chester Anderson's work;[43] Sheldon Brivic's early essays and later his book, *Joyce between Freud and Jung;*[44] and an entire issue of the *James Joyce Quarterly* in 1976.

More contemporary are the poststructuralist, feminist, and marxist studies. Colin MacCabe's *James Joyce and the Revolution of the Word* brought both a post-structuralist and marxist discourse to the novel, attempting to rid it of the encrustations of the Joyce industry.[45] John Paul Riquelme in *Teller and Tale in Joyce's Fiction: Oscillating Perspectives*[46] reopened fruitfully the question of narrative point of view in *Portrait* (and other Joyce works). Others focused criticism on Joyce. Some recent criticism has seemed to argue that we cannot know what Joyce meant or said in his novel. Such a view is based upon the idea that language itself cannot communicate from one mind to another. Phillip Herring's *Joyce's Uncertainty Principle* distinguishes between *indeterminacy*—a condition of all language that precludes knowing what is meant—and *uncertainty*—an "authorial strategy" that introduces "a range of interpretive possibilities."[47] Bonnie Scott, Suzette Henke, and Elaine Unkeless have brought to Joyce another range of interpretive possibilities, informed by feminism.[48] The approach taken to Joyce appears to be dictated as much by our culture's current attitudes, as by something intrinsic and sui generis in Joyce.

The fact that countless persons find Joyce sufficiently interesting and emotionally intriguing to write about him suggests the strength of the novel and the strength of Joyce's imaginary conception of the world. He appears to be one of those touchstones by which we understand and judge our world. Readers have fought with his central character, fought with Joyce's technique, fought with acquiring enough knowledge to read Joyce as a contemporary, or to insist that he is not a contemporary. He matters to hundreds of professional critics and thousands of general readers. I take the continuing professional interest in Joyce and this, his first full-length novel, to be, ultimately a tribute to the power of his story: that that story, whatever it "means," engages readers still, after seventy years.

A READING

Chapter 4

THE VOICES OF THE TEXT AND THEIR STORIES

In 1916, H. G. Wells proclaimed Joyce's new novel "by far the most living and convincing picture that exists of an Irish Catholic upbringing." So it is even today, if we remember that this Irish Catholic grew up before the turn of the century. But Wells didn't stop there: "The technique is startling."[1] And so it is, even today, even after the experimental novels of Virginia Woolf, Samuel Beckett, John Barth, and Gabriel Garcia Marquez. Almost all the criticism of this novel refines or demonstrates the truths of Wells's assertions. My study is no exception. What is "convincing" and what is "startling" about the novel continue to be what interests us as readers.

On the face of it, *Portrait* is simply a realistic tale of a boy growing up in Ireland, in an Irish-Catholic family, during the last part of the nineteenth century. He does what a typical boy might do: he goes to school, initially to a boarding school because of his family's social position (chapter 1); he experiences an initiation into sexuality (chapter 2), becomes tremendously guilt stricken, returns to the Church in his teens, becoming fanatically pious (chapter 3), ultimately loses his faith but gains a new sense of direction (chapter 4), which requires him to kick free of his family—to discover what his life ought to be (chapter 5). The story is told and retold by every generation as every generation faces those patterns of growth and development, and yet each generation feels, somehow, that its experience is unique.

Similarly, the chief questions of everyone's life are Stephen's: Who am I? What am I supposed to do? How can I avoid being destroyed by what seems, at best, an indifferent world, and often indeed a hostile one? Am I any good? These are problems of identity, of worth, of vocation. The very universality of those questions makes the form of the bildungsroman catholic and timeless. We demand, as we read, neither that the hero be exactly like us nor even that the ending be one that is possible in our lives. Almost all novels of development begin with a sense of a past world, for they are all narrated, apparently, after the fact, when the hero is older and, it is hoped, wiser. These are not tales of the here and now, but of the there and then.

However, Wells's comment was not about universality, but rather about the extraordinary realism of *Portrait*—a realism engendered by what another early reviewer saw as new about the novel. Diego Angeli remarked that the novel

> is not so much the narrative of a life as its reminiscence but it is a reminiscence whole, complete and absolute, with all those incidents and details which tend to fix indelibly each feature of the whole. He does not lose time explaining the wherefore of these sensations of his nor even tell us their reason or origin: they leap up in his pages as do the memories of a life we ourselves have lived without apparent cause, without logical sequence. But it is exactly such a succession of past visions and memories which makes up the sum of every life.[2]

The "past visions and memories," as well as their "succession" must be particular—they create the specific not the universal plot.

One trait that distinguishes Joyce's novel from other stories of growth and development is the overtness of *language* as the measuring stick or guide to the protagonist's evolution. Not only do we as readers have only words through which to perceive that evolution (a fact of all novels), and not only does Stephen himself evidence a peculiarly strong interest in words and language, but also the various aspects of his life are imaged as languages spoken often by disembodied voices. Recent literary critics might call these differing languages "discourses"—ways of speaking and shaping utterances that mark the participants as part of a particular conversation.

From the story-telling father who opens the novel to the end of the novel, when Stephen evokes in his own "violent or luxurious language" of revolt (181) the mystical father Daedalus, we know Stephen and he knows himself through the words that define and shape, even create, the realities of his life. In the first chapter, bitter and disruptive languages conflict within Stephen's family, destroying his early childhood illusion of stability and unity. In the second chapter, the language of romantic literature Stephen reads allows him to make heroic sense of his life, while the hell that terrifies him in chapter 3 is wrought purely out of the "words" of Father Arnall and the imagined "language" of the devils. Words may or may not have any necessary relationship to something outside themselves, but in this novel such relationships are overtly denied—words alone exist. Just as hell exists only through Father Arnall's words and the devil's "language," so Stephen's sense of artistic vocation is constructed as the product of his name, another word. "Now . . . his strange name seemed to him a prophecy" (168). As Stephen moves closer and closer to his self-imposed exile, his words form more and more fully the idiosyncratic language he wishes to use as artist rather than assuming any connection with "the reflection of the glowing sensible world" (166). In one sense, such a pattern of language acquisition is regressive; we expect that as children grow up their language will more and more approach the language of their community; Stephen's rejection of his community's languages can be seen not as normal maturation but as a refusal to mature within the boundaries available to him in Ireland at the time of his adolescence. The obverse is equally true: given inadequate cultural languages (what sociologists call symbolic systems and institutions), the healthy individual must create his own. Regression or progression, Stephen's rejections are blatantly dramatized as rejections of languages and voices. Paradoxically, language is used to reject itself.

The culturally given languages, however, mark one way of understanding H. G. Wells's point, for they are the languages of Ireland between about 1885 and 1905. They are spoken, so Stephen believes, by voices (not even people) who intend to destroy his soul: "the constant voices of his father and of his masters" urge a gentlemanly and Catholic life of the sort advocated by Cardinal Newman; "another voice urging him to be strong and manly and healthy" comes from the Irish equivalent of muscular Christianity; "yet another voice had bidden him be true to his country and help to raise up her fallen language and tradition," the language of the Gaelic League and Irish Nationalists; "a worldly voice . . . bid him raise up his father's fallen state"; and "the voice of his school comrades urged him to be a decent fellow" and obtain for them special privileges. "The din of all these hollow-sounding voices" (83–84) threatens at the very least to deafen him. What Stephen turns to is a voice from another world, the world of "phantasmal comrades" who live, largely, in his own imagination, or the voice of "life to his soul not the dull gross voice of the world of duties and despair, not the inhuman voice that had called him to the pale service of the altar" (169), and ultimately, he follows "the voices" that say "We are your kinsmen." In his penultimate diary entry he writes, "They call to me, their kinsman, making ready to go, shaking the wings of their exultant and terrible youth" (252). He moves toward that "spell of arms and voices" (252) as he departs from Ireland, his here and now.

What voices one hears constitute what possibilities the world offers. The tales told by the voices, the possible plots for one's life, determine both goals and means. It is through this din of voices that Stephen Dedalus must make his way to find what is his voice, "some mode of life or art [in which I can express myself] as freely as I can and as wholly as I can" (247). The plot and voices of others limit that wholeness and prevent that freedom. Repetitively, Joyce dramatizes the plight and progress of his hero through the voices, languages, and plots offered to him—those available to a boy in a particular time and place.

To H. G. Wells, one item of "immense significance" about that time and place "is the fact that everyone in this Dublin story, every human being, accepts as a matter of course, as a thing in nature like the sky and the sea, that the English are to be hated." Even when voices and languages in the novel conflict, they agree upon that basic tenet of Irish existence. "It is just hate, a cant," claims the Englishman Wells, "cultivated to the pitch of monomania."[3]

Two political voices and the plots they offer a boy come into conflict in Stephen's life—the nationalist and Catholic voices—but they are initially unified. They are unified in the brushes of Dante Riordan, with one brush for Parnell and one for Davitt; they are unified by the "hate" that Wells disparages. Parnell is most closely associated with parliamentary efforts to win Home Rule for Ireland; Davitt with the Irish Land League. Together they had urged the use of boycotts to fight unfair English landlords. Captain Charles Cunningham Boycott lent his name to the action that threatened to ruin him and other landlords who evicted or gouged tenants. When he needed work done on his land, the native Irish "boycotted" him: they neither harvested nor milled his grain; the blacksmith was unaccountably unable to service his stock; milk maids could not be found to milk his cows. The Land League encouraged such actions and, some claim, more violent attacks upon landlords and those deemed their accomplices.

To understand these two political voices, we have to return to the political background sketched in chapter 1. British parliamentary studies concluded that tax relief and some means of tenants' buying the land they had worked for generations, as well as educational and other agricultural reforms, were crucial. The industrial policies of England had shifted production (and hence jobs) away from the south (the more Catholic portion of Ireland) and to the north. The potato famine had in four years reduced the population of Ireland by 1.5 million people (about 25 percent) in the late 1840s. The capital of the impoverished colony had almost twice the infant mortality rate, worse public sanitation, and triple the unemployment of English cities. Not to be a nationalist, indeed, not to hate England, might be more difficult to conceive of than understanding that monomania of which Wells complains.

What creates for Stephen the distinction between the voice "urging him to be a good catholic above all things" and the voice bidding "him be true to his country and help to raise up her fallen language and tradition" (83, 84) is the split between Davitt and Parnell and the creation of two separate "Irish" voices in response to that split. Stephen's difficulty is not any confusion about being a nationalist, but a confusion generated when faith and secular politics collide.

In the middle of the first chapter the extended family of Stephen Dedalus engages in a futile and destructive argument over politics and religion. The boy, now presumably six or seven, listens to two different languages. Dante preaches what she calls "the language of the Holy Ghost," which condemns the boy's hero, Charles Stewart Parnell, in shrill and ferocious terms. Simon Dedalus and Mr. Casey preach the language of the nationalists, of those who supported Parnell against English intrigue and the Church's condemnation. When the verbal abuse of clerics degenerates into name calling, Stephen's mother pleads, "you should not speak that way before Stephen." But it is an argument that cannot be silenced. Dante seizes the weapon: "—O, he'll remember all this when he grows up . . . the language he heard against God and religion and priests in his own home"(33). Casey counters, "—Let him remember too . . . the language with which the priests and the priests' pawns broke Parnell's heart and hounded him into his grave" (33–34). These languages are presented without explanation, just as a child would have heard them.

The language of the nationalists depends upon a popular and tragic tale of Ireland. It is a tale of innocence betrayed and heroes martyred. In that plot, Ireland—the ancient land of sages and saints as W. B. Yeats had called it—was the center of learning and artistic achievement in the Middle Ages. It was ruled by heroic clans who practiced forms of justice and government remarkably enlightened and democratic. (Remember this is a tale the nationalists told; the historical accuracy of such a tale, even if we thought we could determine it, is irrelevant. What was believed, and what that belief portended for a gifted child is much more central.) Aristocratic heroes and religious faith coexisted, reinforcing each other. That is our donnée for this tale. The action proper begins with Pope Hadrian IV's decision to betray Ireland to the English. In 1155, that only English Pope grants Henry II of England permission to rule in Ireland, a land falsely accused of having fallen away from the true faith. The papal bull thus marks the first betrayal of Ireland as a political unit by the Roman Catholic church, a betrayal of the innocent.

Much of the rest of the story from the time of Henry II to the 1890s mirrors the complicating action of tragedy. It is a tale too long and repetitive to tell in its entirety. For seven hundred years the English ruled and ravaged their colony. The English Renaissance saw increasingly bloody and successful repression of the native Irish: the profitable wine trade with Spain was destroyed by greedy Englishmen who wished the profits of transport and import of wine; English sovereigns saw in the rich forests of Ireland wood they stole and lands they raped. Henry VIII and Elizabeth I imposed on the Catholic peasantry of Ireland tithes to a protestant church they abhorred; both monarchs gave away massive tracks of land to soldiers and courtiers who did not care to live on their newly acquired holdings. Irish law was superseded in favor of English Common Law. Cromwell in the seventeenth century continued the expropriation of land—for "religious" reasons. The absentee landlord, living in England, began to extort the wealth of Ireland, continuing to destroy land and people. The Gaelic language was systematically supplanted by English. When Cromwell and later sovereigns wanted to reward loyal servants, they transported the native Irish to Connaught, a stony region in the west of Ireland and away from the fertile lands of the east and north. Trumped up charges of disloyalty—or so the story went—forced many of these moves; simply being Catholic was sufficient evidence of disloyalty. Under the Penal Laws of the eighteenth century, no priests could be trained or ordained in Ireland; no Catholic child could be educated unless he or she adjured the faith; no judge could be Catholic; no Catholic could hold office; a man with children might be effectively stripped of his ownership rights to land if his senior son was converted to the Protestant, established Church of Ireland (a church in communion with the Church of England). By the 1700s, Catholics controlled only 5 percent of the land of Ireland. The one established university barred Catholics.

Disenfranchised, barred from education and political life as a result of English rule, the Catholics of Ireland nonetheless remained faithful to their church, despite her betrayal of the flock. As Mr. Casey explodes during the Christmas argument, "Didn't the bishops of Ireland betray us in the time of the union when bishop Lanigan presented an address of loyalty to the Marquess Cornwallis?" (38). When Daniel O'Connell won emancipation for Catholics in 1829, he did so at some political cost to Irish nationalism, for he traded Catholic enfranchisement for a general narrowing of the franchise. While he won for Catholics the same voting, property, and educational rights that Protestants enjoyed, he accepted a rise in the property requirements for all voters, so that poorer members of Irish society, whether Protestant or Catholic, could not vote. Such an adjustment cost Catholics more often than Protestants, given the distribution of income between the two denominations. He also confirmed the union with England that denied the separate existence of the Irish nation. In the nationalist plot, the costs were too high; the act benefitted the church but not its members. Mr. Casey continues his analysis and repetition of this story so dear to the hearts of Irish nationalists: "Didn't the bishops and priests sell the aspirations of their country in 1829 in return for catholic emancipation?" (38). The priests, in this tale of Ireland, are not, as Dante claims, "the true friends of Ireland" (38).

This tale of Ireland leads to the nationalists' understanding of the Parnell affair. A colony of England, controlled by English Parliament, betrayed by the very clerics who ought to have protected them, the Irish unsuccessfully rebelled over and over again. The clerics helped suppress the revolution of 1798; they traded power for the people for power for the Church. For the thirty years that preceded Stephen's birth, Irish nationalists had led parliamentary efforts to win the status of Home Rule for Ireland in order to achieve an independent parliament and an independent domestic policy for Ireland. Onto this scene came Charles Stewart Parnell, a figure soon aggrandized into a savior. He fought valiantly for Home Rule, persuading Gladstone to put the issue to a vote in the British Parliament. At the moment of victory, public morality and the English and the Catholic church conspired to dash the hopes of all good Irish. Parnell was named by Captain William O'Shea as corespondent in the divorce suit he brought against Kitty O'Shea. Despite the fact that O'Shea had known of his wife's ten-year infidelity, he waited until an approaching election made Parnell most vulnerable. Some kind of political intrigue, argued the nationalists, determined the timing of his suit. For them, the Catholic church, unable to face a political Irish establishment that might compete with its absolute authority among Catholics, determined to help the English, once again, defeat Irish hopes. It "preach[ed] politics from the altar," threatening excommunication for those who might vote for Parnell, a "public sinner." As it had in the past, it turned *"the house of God into a pollingbooth"* (31). Nationalist language required supporting their leader in his time of need; as Simon Dedalus demands, "Were we to desert him at the bidding of the English people?" (32). The Judas-Church once again dealt the blow.

The denouement is short: Parnell, so the story went, "died of a broken heart" within a year. So ended all hopes for Home Rule, hopes that had inspired the Irish for thirty years. In Stephen's life, the death of Parnell has personal and familial consequences. Simon loses his job and begins an economic descent into abject poverty. His voice explains his decline as resulting from political intrigue; a faithful Parnellite, betrayers and enemies hound him as they had hounded the chief. Whatever hopes Simon had for his son are dashed as surely as Irish hopes for Home Rule were by the death of Parnell. There are personal and cultural reasons that the nationalist voice is so strong in Stephen's imagination.

The voices that call to Stephen to redeem his land and its fallen language call him to redeem the promise of Parnell (the same promise that Wolfe Tone, and the rest of Yeats's "names that stilled your childhood play"[4] had made). In those voices lie the plot that calls for a savior, someone especially chosen "to raise up her [Eire's] fallen language and tradition" (84). Stephen is invited to enact the plot when his peers urge him to join the Gaelic League and the Fenians, a group to which Davin belongs in the last chapter. But the plot proposed by this language—the language of the savior—has within it crucifixion, a possibility that does not escape Stephen. One language he hears in his home is the language of political martyrdom, language that describes a Christ-like savior betrayed by his own people.

Stephen rejects that language. He remembers the fall of Parnell when, some ten years later, his friend urges him to join the Gaelic League, to work for Irish independence. "—No honourable and sincere man," claims Stephen, "has given up to you his life and his youth and his affections from the days of Tone to those of Parnell but you sold him to the enemy or failed him in need or reviled him and left him for another. . . . Ireland is the old sow that eats her farrow" (203). The repetitive, nationalist plot ("from the days of Tone to those of Parnell") and its voices are not for Stephen Dedalus. He indeed remembers, as Mr. Casey hoped he would, "the language of the priests and the priests' pawns" that led to Parnell's untimely death.

If those voices and that language promote a plot for Stephen's life that he rejects, what about the other language, the other voices? These are religious voices, languages, and plots of Stephen's masters, the priests who teach him, of Dante Riordan, and of the Catholic church. That religious language urges him to choose the Church and purity.

In that plot, the Protestant Parnell deserves his punishment; Irish Catholic nationalists should work through Michael Davitt and the Church in their effort to achieve independence. But little constructive action is under way in Catholic nationalist circles—at least in the eyes of Simon Dedalus's son. If the Church cannot offer a story that ends in patriotic success and indeed seems to thwart it, what kind of a story can it offer? The faultless spiritual life, a life culminating in eternal salvation. It offers that life through obedience to its doctrines, through being "a good catholic above all things" (83), and ultimately through the priesthood, a possible climax for the plot of Stephen's life urged in chapter 4. In that plot, Stephen Dedalus would become S. A. Dedalus, S. J. The curve of his life would be dictated by the hours and rituals of the Church. And the return would be power—an outcome the priest who questions Stephen about his vocation highlights:

The Voices of the Text and Their Stories

—To receive that call, Stephen, said the priest, is the greatest honour
that the Almighty God can bestow upon a man. No king or emperor
on this earth has the power of a priest of God. . . . the power of the
keys, the power to bind and to loose from sin, the power of exor-
cism, the power to cast out from the creatures of God the evil spirits
that have power over them, the power, the authority, to make the
great God of Heaven come down upon the altar and take the form
of bread and wine. What an awful power, Stephen! (158)

Even before he determines not to be a priest, Stephen finds the priests
sounding "a little childish in his ears" and he feels "as though he were
slowly passing out of an accustomed world and were hearing its language for the last time" (156). That language of shrill authoritarianism, mimicked in the proffered power of the priest but first heard in
the voice of Dante, is ultimately not the language for Stephen Dedalus.
But Stephen's life does, for some time, follow the voice that urges de-
votion to the Church. Elected head of the Sodality of the Blessed Virgin Mary more than once, his invitation to join the priesthood marks
him as a potential hero in a particular plot. For an Irish Catholic boy
of his generation, such a plot would provide worldly as well as spiritual benefits. As a Jesuit, he would be part of an elite cadre of intel-
lectuals and the life "that awaited him" would be "a life without
material cares" (160). That life, however, threatens "to end for ever,
in time and in eternity, his freedom" (161–62).

His father's voice urges nothing quite so drastic. From the first
chapter on, he urges Stephen always to be a gentleman, never to peach
on a fellow, to be a "bloody good honest Irish[man]" (91), and to mix
only with gentlemen. Stephen's difficulty with his father's suggestions
may stem, as much as anything else, from the absence of money; during Stephen's childhood and adolescence the family falls from relative
prosperity into almost total deprivation.

Here one fictional plot about Ireland affects another possible plot.
Church language destroyed the Dedalus fortune, or so Simon believes;
nationalist language destroyed the ability of the Irish to do anything
independently, as the language of Simon Dedalus with its focus on
betrayers and forces beyond his control makes clear. But the downfall

of Parnell in Simon's constructed story is perhaps most central to the degradation not only of the Dedalus family but of all of Ireland. We see the poverty of the Dedalus family, of Stephen's friends like Lynch, of a flower girl trying to make her living in the streets of Dublin, of students who cannot get jobs: all these represent the denouement of the "uncrowned king's" fall—at least in one possible tale to be told about the "priestridden," "Godforsaken" country. Thus the consequences of the nationalists' plot preclude fulfilling Simon Dedalus's plot to be a gentleman, for neither the Dedaluses' private economy nor the Irish public economy provide the money necessary to that plot. People who cannot buy clothing—or pawn theirs as Stephen's family does in chapter 5—cannot be gentlemen.

The intertwined failures of these plots produce yet another possibility for Stephen Dedalus: the voices that urge him to "raise up his father's fallen state" (84) and repair the family fortune are voices he hears when young. When he wins prize money for his writing, he attempts to fulfill such a plot: "Great parcels of groceries and delicacies and dried fruits arrived from the city. . . . He bought presents for everyone . . . drew up a form of commonwealth . . . opened a loan bank for his family and pressed loans on willing borrowers" (97–98). It fails; the "bank closed its coffers and its books on a sensible loss" (98). Henceforward Stephen knows that that voice urges the impossible. It is "useless" (98). The family's needs outstrip his abilities to produce, especially given his artistic proclivities.

So much will suggest the inadequacy, at least from Stephen's point of view, of the voices that din in his ears and the plots and plans those voices have for his life. As readers we hear these tales and these voices. And as Stephen rejects them, we grow to understand at least why he feels drawn to the voices of his phantasmal comrades, to the voices which at the end of the novel call out to him, "We are alone. Come. . . . We are your kinsmen" (252). These voices, too, must cohere with plots for Stephen's life. Although we may not know those plots, we do know that the cultural voices, the "hollowsounding voices" promise only deafness, not liberation.

The moral and spiritual hollowness, however, is not peculiar to the preformed voices and languages of Stephen's culture. In writing his novel Joyce seems to have assumed what, for the twentieth century, is almost a truism: that there is no "right" way of conducting life, no "right" way of seeing the world; that all of our views of life are constructs, models we put together to make sense of the phenomena of our life. And for Joyce, that putting together was largely rhetorical, having to do with words, not eternal verities, except perhaps (as he told his brother), the love of a mother for her child and the capacity of men to lie.[5] For Joyce life was fiction—a fiction shaped by the human imagination. One could accept someone else's fiction, follow someone else's voice, or shape one's own fiction, discover one's own voice. Thus, Stephen's early and continued interest in language and words foreshadows his artistry, for the literary artist most self-consciously shapes life through language and voice.

As a small child, Stephen shaped language by reshaping—he takes a song that was sung to him by an adult voice and, by changing its words, changes its plot. Stephen remembers: "*O, the wild rose blossoms/On the little green place*. He sang that song. That was his song. *O, the green wothe botheth*" (7). The rose (wothe) is not green in the song, nor does it blossom on the little green place; instead, the "grave" in the original song (almost certainly it was sung around his home) is reshaped to be more positively only a green place, not a grave. (Indeed, while one can imagine *rose* becoming in a child's mouth *wothe*, it is hard to see how the sounds *grave* become *place*.) Reality and the implied plot alter as Stephen alters the words. Later, in math class, Stephen returns to the green rose: "Perhaps a wild rose might be like those colours and he remembered the song about the wild rose blossoms on the little green place. But you could not have a green rose. But perhaps somewhere in the world you could" (12). This vision of something being possible somewhere else corresponds to childhood desires to change by discovering. We might be rich, but the richness would be "found," delivered mysteriously without any action on our part. Ultimately, Stephen wishes to press in his arms "the loveliness that has not yet come into the world" (251); that is, he still wishes to find, to discover or uncover something positive and beautiful that neither his culture nor its voices contain, something beautiful that he and his voice will create.

Even the textures of the novel exhibit this kind of concern for words that shape or create realities. Joyce indicates rhythm and syntax patterns through which Stephen's mind shapes his world. Initially, he learns by comparison and contrast. So in the first pages we learn as Stephen learns that urine is first "warm then it gets cold." Or we learn that his mother "had a nicer smell than his father," or that Uncle Charles and Dante "were older than his father and mother but uncle Charles was older than Dante" (7). We do not learn their ages, a largely irrelevant detail for Stephen; we learn relative things. And only two elements can be compared at any one time: we do not learn that Uncle Charles was the eldest, then Dante, then father, then mother. The Vances "had a different father and mother. They were Eileen's father and mother" (8). The narration makes intellectually simple distinctions, most of which are dualistic: we are not told that, for instance, each family has a different mother and father for this would be generalization from the "facts" of Stephen's experience. We are merely told that his friend has a different mother and father. Piaget would call that concrete operational thinking. The novel forces us to interact with such dualism, such juvenile distinctions. It seems to assume that we will draw the inferences that permit us to "make sense" of the world by weaving our own constructs of the world into those overtly presented in the novel, adding our own to the voices of the novel.

For example, when Stephen is at school, we do not learn that he was scared, but rather that "he kept on the fringe of his line, out of sight of his prefect, out of the reach of the rude feet, feigning to run now and then. He felt his body small and weak amid the throng of players and his eyes were weak and watery" (8). Much of this language, "feigning" or "on the fringe of his line," is not that of a six-year-old. Those are adult words; yet they do not describe what an adult would conclude. Stephen's notions—his eyes were weak and watery—are not the description of an adult who might say, "the child almost cried from unhappiness." The adult would not simply contrast

Stephen with Rody Kickham who "was not like that" (8), as the words of the novel do. The adult would make some evaluative judgment: Stephen was a coward; Stephen was frail; the Kickham boy was a bully. As readers we shift in and out of what Stephen concludes to what an adult voice might say. Much of this occurs without the kind of cuing or warning we expect in a novel. Whose voice is this: "Rody Kickham was not like that: he would be captain of the third line all the fellows said" (8)? The last may be "said" or "thought" by Stephen, but nothing in the novel assigns it to him. We infer a speaker from our own experience of who might shape ideas in this way; the novel cannot even be said to imply our inferences.

What I am describing may be part of what Wells was commenting on when he called Joyce's technique "startling." Unlike traditional novels, we are not told how to add up the precise details. Another way of putting my point comes from Diego Angeli in a passage I've already quoted: Joyce "does not lose time explaining the wherefore of these sensations of his or even tell us their reason or origin: they leap up in his pages as do the memories of a life we ourselves have lived without apparent cause, without logical sequence. But it is exactly such a succession of past visions and memories which makes up the sum of every life."[6] As readers, we work to explain the why or wherefore of these sensations, and as we explain we shape and create our own version or fiction, our own plot of this novel.

In subsequent chapters I suggest some of the ways we can shape and re-create the novel, hearing what voices come to us and bringing—necessarily—our own voices and plots to those of the novel.

Chapter 5

"ONCE UPON A TIME . . .": FAIRY TALES AND READERS' EXPECTATIONS

Approaching Joyce's *A Portrait of the Artist as a Young Man* for the first time, we may well be bewildered by this classic that starts with peculiarly odd and yet familiar language: "Once upon a time and a very good time it was there was a moocow coming down along the road and this moocow that was coming down along the road met a nicens little boy named baby tuckoo" (7). The opening immediately disrupts our expectations. This is not, we know, a child's story, yet so many of our childhood stories begin with "once upon a time. . . ." We make guesses that allow us to continue reading. If we shut the book, we've probably made a guess that goes something like, "oh, I got the wrong book," or "this is stupid." But to continue reading we must bring to the words some way of mediating between our expectations and the reality that faces us, the "classic" that opens with a classic fairy tale formula.

The novel starts with an unidentified voice (and perhaps an unidentifiable one) telling the kind of story whose formulaic beginning promises a formulaic ending. While we assume that some adult is telling this children's story, even that assumption seems uncertain. Surely Stephen's father, Simon Dedalus, does not say "met a nicens little boy," though any parent might indeed be guilty of "moocow," in that odd way adults have of teaching by corrupting, a practice that goes back at least to the Renaissance when Edward Hake proposed talking like a child to children as a teaching technique. We know, almost instantly, that we do not have a narrator who will explain or make sense of the story he tells. Colin MacCabe in *James Joyce and the Revolution of the Word* argues that Joyce's use of language denies us our "normal" ability to define ourselves as superior to the events and characters of a novel, where we—like the narrator—"know" more. Earlier, "traditional" stories in his view place "us in a position of dominance with regard to the stories and characters." And that happens because the narrative prose of what MacCabe calls classic realist texts claims "to grant direct access to a final reality."[1] But here, at the beginning of Joyce's novel, what is the "final reality"? And how are we to know it if it, like the moocow, comes down along the road to meet us?[2] Other commentators have used different language to describe the same experience. For Hugh Kenner, the narrative voice is neither Stephen, nor his father, nor a traditional narrator.[3]

One way of making sense of this story is to take our cue from the opening and assume that this story is to be like a fairy tale. Perhaps like those stories of our past, it will have a way of making possible the impossible or making tolerable the intolerable. We remember, for instance, that Little Red Riding Hood survives ingestion by the Big Bad Wolf. The generalized plot of a fairy tale is familiar. This voice, then, in its choice of form suggests a particular kind of plot, just as the voices of nationalist- and religious-proposed plots.

Traditional fairy tales concern small and often threatened beings (not always human) who are orphaned, deserted, or separated from their proper parents (stepparents are frequently wicked substitutes). Through a series of adventures, these small beings find help from supernatural beings who provide the means of triumphing over undeserved threats. Threats come without reason: Why are stepmothers so wicked? Why does the wolf wish to eat Little Red Riding Hood? Why does the witch wish Hansel and Gretel harm? And the fairy godmother or the animal who magically speaks to the child helps for no reason other than the hero's goodness and the supernatural being's nature. The hero will be rewarded only if he dares to do the impossible; in Bruno Bettelheim's words, these plots "promise that if the child dares to engage in this fearsome and taxing search, benevolent powers will come to his aid, and he will succeed."[4] Finally, the formulaic beginning is matched by a formulaic ending of survival and happiness, "and they lived happily ever after."

The opening of Joyce's story, then, lets us hope that the impossible can be possible, that the small and marginal may survive against the big, and old, and central, or that the private voice and its desires can triumph over the powerful voices of authority, voices that contain threats. However foolish Little Red Riding Hood was—and however foolish our hero of this book might turn out to be—we would, should we have to choose, support and identify with the small girl against the wolf, and with Stephen Dedalus against older and threatening voices that direct him and attempt to control his childhood and adolescence. It is, after all, "his story," as the first page of the novel tells us. He is the artist as a young man.

Such a view or context for the opening of this novel is reinforced by arbitrary threats made to Stephen Dedalus before we finish the second page of the novel. Stephen apparently proposes marriage to another toddler, Eileen Vance, and then hides under the table. Immediately after that action, Stephen is told that he will apologize,"—O, if not, the eagles will come and pull out his eyes" (8). We cannot determine what his error has been (Deciding to marry Eileen? Hiding under the table? Doing something else that prompted him to hide under the table?). We cannot determine what Stephen has done because the words of the story do not tell us—though at least two possible "crimes" are indicated.

Not only does this bizarre threat match the equally bizarre dangers of fairy tales, but also the lack of clear motive for the threat matches fairy-tale plots that similarly ignore linear, causal plot sequences. Why do Cinderella's stepmother and stepsisters hate her? Why would a wolf eat a grandmother or a small child? What crime has Stephen committed? Why would eagles choose to blind such an unimportant being as a child hiding under a table? No matter. Some malevolent force will descend upon him to pull out his eyes if he doesn't obey what must seem irrational commands of his elders. For Bettelheim, traditional fairy tales reassure the child who feels impotent and threatened, and tales do this, in part, by accepting as true the fears that adults erroneously label "irrational" or "false."[5] In that way, these stories reassure the child that his or her view is not wrong or culpable, but justified. Children *are* eaten by wolves. Stephen may, indeed, believe the eagles *will* pull out his eyes.

Adult readers may suppose that the crime must be sexual, coming as it does right after his announced intention to marry Eileen; some readers strengthen the case by arguing that the blinding is a sublimated form of castration because eyes have some connection to knowing or seeing and hence to carnal knowledge or voyeurism. But the "real" causal connection between the specified punishment and the unspecified crime is left to the reader to supply. Just like those causal connections in fairy tales. And just like those connections made by children who feel the world and its voices to be arbitrary and inexplicable. To escape those arbitrary powers, the child requires magic or some benevolent power that is benevolent not because the child deserves it but because it simply is, of its nature, benevolent.

As Stephen identifies with the story's character, he chooses the story as his, just as most children choose particular stories. Each has one or more that capture his or her emotional situation and intuitively the child identifies with a character. "The content," says Bettelheim, "of the chosen tale usually has nothing to do with the patient's external life, but much to do with his inner problems," allowing a "voyage into the interior of [his] mind, into the realms of unawareness."[6] If, then, this tale captivates Stephen (as it did his creator), it must resonate to the inner concerns of the fictional character. To understand Stephen, we can profitably inquire what emotional conflicts the story might resonate to. At the same time, we are being told stories, too—a story of a child being told a story, a story of a child remembering being told a story, a story of a moocow and a nicens little boy. And if we find the stories resonating to our inner problems, we may find ourselves both in and out of those stories. Like children who listen to a fairy tale and choose to identify with its hero, as readers we engage in an analogous and dynamic act. If, for instance, we too feel threatened by the voices of authority that seem to limit our freedom and creativity, we may find Stephen's story resonating to our own—and we may "make" Stephen's story ours. But as we do so, we shape or change that "external" story to suit our inner story, adding our voice to "make sense" of the tale told.

Just what is the "told" story of the moocow and baby tuckoo is not known. The moocow, in traditional Irish faery tales, can be one of "the faery." Cows in general are associated with Ireland, a symbol of her land and people, and moocows are female and potentially nurturing, and might, therefore, look for that nicens little boy who is both baby tuckoo and Stephen. Donal Gifford in *Joyce Annotated* maintains that the story tells of children transported by a "supernatural (white) cow . . . across to an island realm where they are relieved of the petty restraints and dependencies of childhood and adolescence and magically schooled as heroes before they are returned to their astonished parents and community."[7] The cow may be, therefore, one of Bettelheim's "benevolent powers" come to aid the small child. There is biographical evidence for seeing this story as a traditional, Irish faery tale: John Stanislaus Joyce wrote his son James on his forty-ninth birthday, "I wonder do you recollect the old days in Brighton Square, when you were Babie Tuckoo, and I used to take you out in the Square and tell us all about the moo-cow that used to come down from the mountain and take little boys across?"[8] Some recent commentators have tried to establish the particular time when John Joyce told this tale, claiming that the tale is one of oedipal punishment for the son's desiring of the mother and told as she delivered a subsequent child.[9] Yet that understanding of the story does not account for the apparently repetitive telling of the tale of the moocow and baby tuckoo. John Joyce's letter makes it clear that he told the story more than once ("I used to take you out . . .") and certainly suggests that the tale was one that amused or delighted his son sufficiently for the father to remember years later the context and the tale. And Stephen? The evidence we have—that is, the words of Joyce's novel—equally claims the story as "his": "He was baby tuckoo" (7).

Gifford claims that the story resembles tales "still current in Ireland," and therefore for a "child" of Joyce's contemporary years, "known." We require information out of that stockpile of "scholarship" of earlier stories. The "faery" as Irish folklore creatures are infamous kidnappers; Yeats's "The Stolen Child" tells one such story where the faery urge the child away from a "world more full of weeping than you can understand."[10] They had the power to reward or to punish. To be "taken across," in John Joyce's phrase, might indeed suggest a journey to the faery kingdom. To what end? Assuming Gifford's identification is right, to the end that the small child might, through the intervention of a good animal (a typical folklore motif), be saved from destruction and just as important, be made worthy or good. A child threatened with blinding eagles for some vaguely understood crime might wish for such a transfiguration or rescue, and so the story might well resonate to inner needs, suggesting as it does that one might escape punishment and ultimately escape the wickedness (one's own) that prompted the threat.

The first section of chapter 1 ends with the threatened Stephen hiding under the table. Whether he ever apologized is left to our imaginations. When the scene abruptly switches—after the asterisks—from the potentially blinding eagle to the playground of Clongowes Wood School, we are faced with additional decisions about plot. Is Stephen sent away because he did not apologize? Or, alternatively, does he think he has been sent away for this unnamed crime? Are we to connect the two scenes at all? Stephen's position in the two scenes is similar: in each he appears threatened by larger, implacable (How does one apologize for an unspecified error?), malevolent creatures. These are the kinds of threats we find in all fairy tales. And it is this sense of threat that associates the two scenes, allowing us to make a transition, despite the text's inability to name the causal relationship between the two situations.

Indeed, when we "arrive" at the boarding school, we are not given any conclusion about Stephen's feelings or experiences. No narrator tells us that Stephen feels homesick or scared or threatened. No interior monologue from Stephen's point of view makes that point. Instead we are shown, or we join, a scene to which we bring our own experiences of life and conclude that Stephen is homesick and frightened:

> The wide playgrounds were swarming with boys. All were shouting and the prefects urged them on with strong cries. The evening air was pale and chilly and after every charge and thud of the footballers the greasy leather orb flew like a heavy bird through the grey light. He kept on the fringe of his line, out of sight of his prefect, out of the reach of the rude feet, feigning to run now and then. He felt his body small and weak amid the throng of players and his eyes were weak and watery. Rody Kickham was not like that: he would be captain of the third line all the fellows said. (8)

The words threaten: people swarm, charge, shout, throng; they have rude feet (both rough and unpleasant?), the football itself is ugly—greasy. Like the smallest child anywhere and like the small children of fairy tales, the hero is outnumbered and clearly marginal or self-marginalizing, keeping "on the fringe of his line," away from the others, and disguising his separation. What he feels is a hopeless, because causeless, condition of being himself, weak and small. But it is his body, not himself, that is labeled weak. And he is not crying; his eyes, as though separate from him, are "watery" as well as being, like his body, weak. One point here is that the threats are both external to our hero and internal or intrinsic. Throughout this second section of the first chapter, Stephen feels that he is wrong, out of place, marginal. The boys inquire after his father and instantly we are told that he "crept about from point to point on the fringe of his line" (9); he sees himself afraid not of the boys but of their now animated eyes and boots: "Jack Lawton's yellow boots dodged out the ball and all the other boots and legs ran after" (10). Except Stephen's boots and legs. Although Stephen (not his boots) does run for a bit, he gives up: "It was useless to run on. Soon they would be going home for the holidays" (10). Just as trees and animals talk in children's stories, so too in this novel boots and legs threaten. One boy shoulders "him into the square ditch" containing sewage because he won't "swop his little snuffbox for Wells's seasoned hacking chestnut" (10). And Stephen feels, repeatedly, that he doesn't know the "right answer"—the condition of the hero in fairy tales who cannot know without help.

The boys taunt him, especially the villain Wells who shouldered him into the ditch: "—Tell us, Dedalus, do you kiss your mother before you go to bed?" Like riddles in traditional tales, this one has no apparent answer. First Stephen says yes, only to be laughed at. Then he changes his mind and says "I do not" only to be laughed at again. "What was the right answer to the question? He had given two and still Wells laughed." Stephen here focuses on one boy—or perhaps Joyce focuses only on one boy—an arch villain in our fairy-tale analogue despite the fact that they "all laughed" (14). Like the tales Bettelheim discusses, this tale paints the antagonist darkly, clearly, unambivalently. The persecutor gets his just reward when Stephen falls sick, perhaps because of his treatment. Wells is scared, the tables are turned. Wells sneaks back into the empty dormitory to beseech Stephen, "Don't spy on us, sure you won't?" (21). The *us* is either slang or a misuse of the plural, for all are convinced that Wells was the villain. Our hero triumphs through his digestive system; his illness has vanquished the villain. Stephen can from his point of view as a school boy imagine only one way to triumph irrevocably over his enemy: he could die and then "Wells would be sorry . . . for what he had done" (24).

The oddest element of Stephen's fantasy that his death will overcome his enemies lies in the parallel he constructs between his martyred state and the martyred state of his hero, Charles Stewart Parnell. The parallel suggests that Parnell, too, is a figure in a fairy tale, a small and marginal being attacked and threatened by large, malevolent voices of England and the Roman Catholic church. If physical illness becomes the benevolent power that will allow Stephen to triumph, so analogously Parnell's death seems to Stephen to be that special, supernatural event that will make his world right, coherent, stable again, solving the problems and the threats of familial disruption that he feels are brought about by politics.

Ireland's uncrowned king and his father's hero, Parnell, dies while

Stephen lies ill at school. For Stephen, the betrayal (or rejection) of Parnell is most vividly dramatized by Dante Riordan who "had ripped the green velvet back off the brush that was for Parnell one day with her scissors and had told him that Parnell was a bad man" (16). He had in that earlier passage "wondered if they were arguing at home about that. That was called politics" (16). That domestic fight eventuates in (or at least precedes) Parnell's death, just as Stephen imagines his fight with Wells will eventuate in his death. In Stephen's father's view (and his own), Parnell and Stephen are equally innocent in the fight. Thus, by the emotional logic of fever, his death would make Wells sorry and Parnell's death would make Dante sorry. Both plots are the stuff of fairy tales. Thus, the second section ends not just with Stephen's temporary triumph over his classmate Wells through his own imaginary death, but also with Dante "in a maroon velvet dress and with a green velvet mantle . . . walking proudly and silently past the people who knelt by the waters' edge" to greet Parnell's coffin (27). The green velvet, so rudely ripped off, returns, signifying Dante's reconciliation to the chief.

At that point of triumph we shift abruptly to Stephen's promised land, home, for Christmas. Stephen is back from his first exile, his first potential visit to the faery kingdom. But his initiation into that other world has not prepared him for the rupture that occurred while he was gone—or for its aftermath. As his people argue about Charles Stewart Parnell, Stephen in terror watches his father cry and his pseudo aunt scream like a harridan. Apparently the fairy-tale reconciliation has not worked.

The transformed being discovers that neither his own imaginary death nor Parnell's real death has managed to make his world safe. During the Christmas dinner that highlights Stephen's longed-for vacation, such fantasies are rudely shaken: Parnell's death has only intensified Dante's animosity. Stephen returns from Clongowes with that magical transformation of the faery kingdom; he looks grown-up and is allowed to join the adults for Christmas dinner while the children remain upstairs in the nursery. It is, as Stephen had imagined, perfect. It is warm as opposed to the cold of his school. His mother is elegant and his father, the storyteller who (if we follow Gifford's identification) promised this transfiguration through an exile to faeryland, tells new stories, "with the voice of the hotelkeeper" (29) to the delight of his son.

But the idyll explodes as the family wrangles through the old political fight. Did Parnell, through his adultery with Kitty O'Shea, give up his right to Irish support? Were the priests and bishops right to attack him and overturn the best chance Ireland had to achieve Home Rule? Or were Mr. Casey and Simon right that it was merely one more instance of the Church betraying the political aspirations of Ireland, of confusing religion with politics, of presuming to turn the house of God into a polling booth? Stephen sits in terror watching the world that he thought so wonderful reduced to a screaming match in which two voices—one speaking the language of political need and the other of religious orthodoxy—tear at each other until, like the languages from the Tower of Babel, one cannot hear or understand the other. Dante screams: "—Devil out of hell! We won! We crushed him to death! Fiend!" and Casey sobs, "—Poor Parnell! . . . My dead king!" and Simon Dedalus's "eyes were full of tears" (39).

Abruptly section 3 ends, signified by the asterisks across the page that provide no information about what causes the next scene or even the denouement of the previous one. In our fairy-tale plot, Stephen was to acquire some special power of understanding or skill; yet the fight at Christmas indicates that the secrets learned in Stephen's earlier triumphs were not enough. The unacceptable terror of his Christmas breaks off into silence; no voice records the truth. We are left as we are so often, to fill in the space, to conclude from so little, what Stephen makes of the scene, and what we are to make from it. Section 1 ended in much the same way we may remember—with Stephen under the table, threatened by the women of his household. Here he looks up (as he must have done from his vantage point beneath the table) and sees his father's eyes full of tears.

Another exile begins instantly in our reading time; Stephen is transported back to Clongowes where, immediately, the confusion of Christmas seems transposed into confusion of another kind at the school. Someone has done something wrong; some boys have been caught "smugging," a mysterious act to Stephen and one that the novel is at some pains to keep mysterious. But the threat, again, is real to Stephen and to the other boys who worry that "we are all to be punished for what other fellows did" (43). Similarly, what Parnell did created the punishment of continued British rule for all Ireland—and, perhaps, the declining prosperity of the Dedalus family. To these new threats Stephen must respond—most concretely to the threat of being punished for something someone else may have done but that he did not do.

Stephen, in an apparently unrelated incident, breaks his glasses, ostensibly an innocent if careless act. But Father Dolan, finding Stephen not doing his schoolwork during class, pandies him publicly. Stephen may, indeed, have received the fall-out from the sins of the other boys. But the cause of Father Dolan's malevolence, like that of Wells and Dante earlier, is unspecified. The three tormentors share a kind of Iago-like malevolence; in no case does Stephen "deserve" his treatment. When Father Dolan pandies the child accusing him of being an idler and a schemer, Stephen's quandary is clear. Either the supposed good people (the adults) are not good—and he is being mistreated—or he is an idler. Attempting to find a third possibility, one that reconciles his trust in the priests and his sense of himself, he imagines that although innocent he may look guilty: "He suffered time after time in memory the same humiliation until he began to wonder whether it might not really be that there was something in his face which made him look like a schemer and he wished he had a little mirror to see" (53). He begins to assume that he must be wrong in some way that he cannot control. It is no wonder that this child might find the arbitrariness of fairy tales resonant to his own experiences.

Reminded by other stories of people who had been great and who had escaped unfair punishment, Stephen determines to seek help to find what Bettelheim called "benevolent powers that will come to his aid,"[11] and so his benevolent power—Conmee—does. Daring to cross the divide between his world and that outer, adult world, Stephen leaves the other boys and goes on a long journey into the recesses of the castle. It is like other trips in other tales, a cold, dark trip that requires courage. Stephen hesitates, wondering if hiding is not the better course to take because "when you were small and young you could often escape that way" (55). But he goes, down the narrow dark corridor, up the stairs, past the pictures of other heroes and saints (we are all heroes of our own story), to Father Conmee who does indeed promise to prevent Stephen's persecution at the hands of Father Dolan. And so the small person once more triumphs over the larger and more central person; this time with help from literature, and his own brain, not his stomach. Conflict in fairy tales arises from the possibility that evil persons will win; the hero is rewarded only if he dares to do the impossible, as Stephen has dared to attack the hierarchy of his school. Unfortunately, he does not live happily ever after. Chapter 1 provides only one adventure in his tale.

One more possible parallel between fairy tales and this story lies in Stephen's repeated need for benevolent, external powers. Stephen makes two voyages out from home, both imposed upon him by adults, both challenging his own sense of worth, and both allowing him to triumph through some external power, his own illness or Father Conmee's intervention. Unfortunately, however triumphant he is away from home, home itself is threatened by forces Stephen understands no better than he understands Dante's threatening eagles, his classmate's malevolence, or Father Dolan's belief that he is evil. Returning home again, after the triumph of Clongowes and the vanquishing of his third adversary, Stephen is left but little time to savor his triumph, for new faces or voices once again threaten in chapter 2 to destroy his sense of worth and competence, earned so dearly at his boarding school.

When Stephen is punished for breaking his glasses, he may indeed have received the fall-out of the other boys' smugging; when, in chapter 2 it becomes clear that Simon Dedalus has lost his job, he may have received the fall-out from Parnell's crime. To these threats, and actual punishment in Stephen's case, Stephen responds by seeking a higher benevolent power that can and will protect him from malevolent forces.

This pattern of salvation externalizes the saving grace just as fairy tales do. And in Stephen's life, various external saviors work in his behalf. At the end of chapter 1, Stephen seeks and receives help from Father Conmee, the rector of Clongowes. In chapter 2, he is led by "a premonition" that "the unsubstantial image which his soul so constantly beheld . . . would, without any overt act of his, encounter him" (65). That is, some sacred moocow would come down along a road and meet Stephen, baby tuckoo, and transform him: "Weakness and timidity and inexperience would fall from him in that magic moment" (65). In chapter 2, the moocow in the form of a prostitute meets him. As "he stood still in the middle of the roadway. . . . A young woman dressed in a long pink gown laid her hand on his arm to detain him and gazed into his face" (100). She initiates a marvelous transformation of Stephen into a being "strong and fearless and sure of himself" (101).

In chapter 3 religious salvation, first seen as a threat, similarly encounters Stephen with no overt act of his: "Stephen's heart had withered up like a flower of the desert that feels the simoom coming from afar" (108). The Christ "born in a poor cowhouse" (118) comes, calling "to men to hear the new gospel" (118). And, after his confession "the ciborium had come to him" (146), as newly arisen he finds transformation, "relieved of the petty restraints of childhood and magically schooled."[12] In chapter 4, Stephen "meets" with a girl on the beach who seems to certify his sense of calling as an artist; she comes unbeckoned, and aids in yet another transformation.

But each of these transformations, like that at the end of chapter 1, is transient, destroyed by the events of home and fatherland and, except for chapter 3, mother church. The novel ends with Stephen journeying out to meet the transformer—to go to the voices of his youth that call to him and claim they are his kindred. Even at the end of the novel, Stephen Dedalus looks for that journey across, the journey that promises transfiguration.

Indeed, the story of the promised moocow can be seen as always "his story," the story of a being magically removed from the mundane and petty and brought into knowledge and skill and power, much to the bewilderment of his parents and community. In chapter 5, Stephen's mother, bewildered by his behavior and his growth at the university, complains without much analysis: "—Ah, it's a scandalous shame for you, Stephen, . . . and you'll live to rue the day you set your foot in that place [University College, Dublin]. I know how it has changed you" (175). Shortly before his father asked, has that "lazy bitch of a brother gone out yet?" (175). It is certainly true that Stephen's family treats him as somehow different and special, as though filled with that *virtu* promised by the moocows that spirit away the children of Ireland: "All that had been denied [his brothers and sisters] had been freely given to him, the eldest: but the quiet glow of evening showed him in their faces no sign of rancour" (163). Rather than working to aid the financial disrepair of his family, Stephen goes to university and escapes, ultimately to the Continent. He is not like those who must earn their keep, constrained by the mundane and ordinary facts of this, rather than the faery, world.

The context "fairy tales," then, can shape our reading of this novel from start to finish, helping us create a tale of threat, intercession, transfiguration. Rarely do we as readers work out as consciously as I am suggesting here what the consequences of our first guess might be. And yet, when we read, we do carry with us initial impressions and connections to make sense of or to navigate within the story. Our understanding of Mark Twain's *Huckleberry Finn*, for instance, depends upon our initial assumptions and impressions of the voice that tells us on the first page how "rough" it was living with someone as "dismal regular and decent" as the widow, in what we take to be nonstandard English.[13] That voice is obviously not Mark Twain's, and we expect some difference between the attitudes expressed by this child's voice and the attitudes of the author. The text does not tell us that such a difference exists. We create its truth, the truth of a world constructed by a young boy. Similarly, for some of Joyce's readers, seeing this tale as part of a larger tradition of fairy tales, may help create meaning and order where the text fails to supply it.

The absence of clear and definite clues in the text, however, can lead us to make different and differing assumptions about the story.

Even those readers who agree that the fairy-tale opening is significant may reach different conclusions. For instance, we might, instead, think of fairy tales as adult manipulation. After all, the threats they propose terrify as clearly as their endings console. Bruno Bettelheim's argument that fairy tales and tales of magic function to control the threatening aspects of the external world appears one-sided. While most children learn these tales and take solace, the tales are told by the parents and adults who appear to control the child and the world, and who are therefore part of the threat. Curiously, Joyce's tale and many others create a world in which the child is orphaned or separated from the parents, surely not a situation of comfort and solace. Why would any parent raise such fears in a child? Why do parents tell these tales of supernatural beings who disrupt the lives of small animals or small boys and girls? If we take Simon Dedalus's tale again, why does he want to suggest that a moocow (a rather large and imposing creature) might spirit the child away from the world he knows? And why, in Joyce's tale, is it the father with a hairy face that tells the tale? The first page of *Portrait* tells us that Stephen's father looks at him through a glass—perhaps the glasses or monocle that we later discover Simon wears. Is there in that image a sense of threat?

Such a view of how the fairy-tale opening helps create meaning in this story coheres with other, and negative views of Stephen's father as storyteller. Edmund Epstein, recalling the Joycean epiphany[14] upon which the threat was based, points out that James Joyce was terrified by Eileen Vance's father who claimed James had to apologize or the eagles would pull out his eyes. Epstein argues that Dante's phrase "the eagles will come and pull out his eyes" echoes a scriptural passage that threatens a son for mocking his father and despising his mother—" 'let the raven of the brooks pick [the eye] out, and the young eagles eat it.'" That is, for Epstein, the threats are threats against a child who does not obey the father, here "represented" by Dante. "The biblical verse-paraphrase in the text, shifted from Mr. Vance to Aunt Dante, relates the punishment of a son who scorns and defies his parents."[15]

Colin MacCabe proposes that "the narrating father . . . fixes one in place with his look and his story ('he was baby tuckoo'),"[16] limiting and controlling Stephen through his voice and narrative, denying Stephen's separateness, as we might fix a bug with a straight pin. If we respond in ways similar to MacCabe, we may consider other parallel tales in trying to understand the opening. The father stares at his child and tells him a terrifying story of being transported away from home by a cow. Stephen, as an Irish child, might well understand the world of the faery as many Irish tales have it—an amoral world to which children are often kidnapped, never to return to their own world. For the Irish faery are not human; they exist separately from the constraints of human society; they may torment as easily as aid. In Yeats's "The Stolen Child," the child—after irrevocably going with the faeries—gazes back not to a world filled with weeping but to an inviting, nurturing human world. And if the moocow is female, then the idea of being kidnapped by a source of milk and taken away from the lemon platt of Betty Byrne may not be appealing. Is Simon proposing exile for his child? Isn't it possible that, whatever Simon consciously intends, he is suggesting punishment? Later Stephen sees the winter pasture of moocows and finds their dung so repulsive that he doesn't wish to drink their milk. And the child who leaves Ireland at the end of the novel because, in part, she is "the old sow that eats her farrow" (203) may have conflicting responses to the female nurturer even if she is supernatural. Ireland does seem to Stephen to attempt to kidnap him from his proper mission: Ireland is one of the "nets flung at" his soul to "hold it back from flight" (203), one of the "hollowsounding voices" that din in his ear (84), to prevent his own choosing. If we follow this curve of logic, we can see Stephen's *active* seeking of transforming power—his decision to leave Ireland, to escape the father who threatens with faery cows—as his first healthy move.

There are, of course, other ideas or experiences we bring to this novel to make it ours, to remake it in our own image. What is crucial is the sense that Joyce's novel seems to invite conflicting "senses" in its readers, denying us certainty about what the author meant.

Most readers, for instance, have seen the first two pages of the novel as an overture that introduces major motifs and concerns like the overture to a symphony or light opera. But that is a "constructed" understanding of the first two pages: it requires that we know operas or symphonies, it requires that, having finished the book, we see the major motifs building first in this section, it requires that we read in particular ways with particular understandings of some kind of tradition, what some readers are now calling the *intertext*. Similarly, to connect the fairy tale of page 7 to the fairy tale John Joyce refers to in his letter requires that we know words associated closely with Joyce's life written by his father. Even connecting the opening with other fairy tales requires that we know fairy tales—and know that they share words in a particular position in the story. In one sense, then, I've been urging attending to one kind of intertext, one series of relationships between these words and their prior use, these words and the category of tales labeled "fairy."

If, instead, we start with the response "overture," a response that cannot occur on the first line, or probably on the first two pages, we begin to have other expectations—expectations that operate, largely, on second readings of the novel. So, for instance, we can say that Dante's pin with its red brush for Michael Davitt and its green brush for Charles Stewart Parnell (called only Parnell in the text) "introduces" the political conflicts within the Dedalus family only after one has read the whole novel. On first reading, they call up issues that an Irish person in 1916 would know, however. And those issues of nationalism (Parnell) and land reform (Michael Davitt) become, as we read, issues of religion—of the power of the Catholic priests to intervene in the politics of a nation and of the English domination of Ireland that affects Stephen Dedalus and all members of his society. These are, in Yeats's phrase, "names that stilled your childish play,"[17] names that resonated for the Irish. If we place these particular words in that word hoard, we find ourselves focused on Stephen's political situation—and see him as the underclass in the opening of the novel, unaware of the issues raised by the symbolic items of his home, but clearly and definitely aware of his own impotence. Hiding under the table to escape the claws of the eagles is analogous to his attempts to escape from the rude boots of the larger boys on the playground, and those two personal, political situations are analogous to the powerful clergy's hounding of Parnell and to Father Dolan's pandying of Stephen, and so on. That is, we can focus on all the instances in the novel of authorities persecuting others.

Reading the first chapter with a focus on political issues brings out sexual possibilities in the text, and like focusing on the fairy tale, this perspective has biographical/editorial bases. Hans Walter Gabler pointed out that the composition of the first chapter reveals Joyce changing his own focus by moving the Christmas dinner scene from chapter 2 back into chapter 1 and focusing on the boys' impotence vis-á-vis their teachers in the second Clongowes Wood's scene.[18] It is possible to argue that the fall of Parnell for sexual errors makes the teachers more strident with the boys and less fair. It is clear, I think, that the sin of the boys caught in smugging is associated with Stephen's potential sexual error vis-à-vis Eileen in section 1 of the chapter, and that motif of sexual transgression echoes to Parnell's fall. Readers can, thus, focus on sexual transgression and the response authority makes to that transgression, constructing a story of psychological manipulation.

What we make of this story, then, depends on how we focus and what we bring—what stories and plots and words—to our reading of the story. Although readers share the particular words of the novel, we may differ in our interpretations both because we each attribute meaning to words in personal ways and because words themselves are not fixed or definite in meaning. The novel can be read as fairy tale, as a political and social analysis of Ireland in the late nineteenth century, as a psychological study of young children or of artistic young children, as an analysis of the effects of Catholicism, etc. The inferences we draw are as at least as much our own as they are what Joyce implies; we cannot be certain what he, or any other author, implies.

Chapter 6

STORYTELLERS AND PATRIARCHY: FROM SIMON DEDALUS TO FATHER DAEDALUS

When, at the end of the novel, Stephen announces to himself and to his readers his departure from Ireland, he proclaims an ancestry: "27 *April:* Old father, old artificer, stand me now and ever in good stead" (253). The novel begins with a biological father (if we can speak of characters having a biology); it ends with an appeal to an imaginative father, Daedalus. Like the other voices of Stephen's childhood and adolescence, the voice of the storytelling father proposes plots, conditions, and attitudes for the young Stephen. As flesh-and-blood sons do, Stephen looks first to his father to provide his identity and his values; our fathers, especially if we be male children, are our first authorities. The voice of the father who biologically authors him is rejected as Stephen chooses, throughout the book, new fathers with their voices and their plots—ultimately choosing the new, "old father, old artificer" Daedalus (253).

One father opens this story with his story; another father closes it. The biological father is displaced by the chosen father, the latter invoked almost as a patron saint at the end, as Stephen Dedalus seeks to fly to the voices that call, "we are your kinsmen" (252). Between these two poles, however, other fathers populate Stephen's world: his religious fathers (Dolan, Conmee, Arnall, and a host of nameless clerics), the fatherland of Ireland, and more literary fathers—some of whom are also "fathers of the Church," with Thomas Aquinas being the most central of them. Stephen's journey could be seen as a quest for the father of his choice, an odd and paradoxical phrase in itself. We cannot choose our fathers, in one sense. They pre-exist us. We certainly cannot choose our biological fathers, whatever the adolescent desire may be. Stephen's sense, by the second chapter, that he is a "fosterchild" (98) to his parents stands as but one indication of his desire to do so. Just as crucially, we cannot choose the "pool" of metaphoric fathers. They are the givens of our culture; they are *auctors,* the Latin word from which our words, author, authority, authorize descend. An *auctor* is a creator, a progenitor, a father, as well as a writer. (So, for instance, we speak of Einstein as the author of relativity or the founding fathers as the authors of our liberties.) And we cannot choose what progenitors precede us, but we can and do choose from that pool, selecting those "elders" who best respond to our own needs and proclivities. We choose mentors, influences, philosophical guides; such choices involve rejecting other guides, other mentors, other fathers. Taking our cue from the opening and closing fathers, we can make one kind of sense of this novel by focusing on the fathers Stephen chooses and rejects.

THE LIMITS OF BIOLOGY: SIMON DEDALUS

In this massively male novel, Stephen's quest for identity focuses almost exclusively on the males he seeks either to identify with or to reject. In the first chapter, Stephen perceives his world as simple. Obedience to the clerical fathers at Clongowes and to his biological father at home guarantees success. But fathers turn out not to be so simple a matter. Simon Dedalus becomes suspect, potentially unsatisfactory, because of his social position as soon as Stephen leaves his home. When the boys at Clongowes ask, "—What is your father?" Stephen responds "a gentleman" (9). But, in that distinctive style of *Portrait,* the matter is immediately confused, for the inquisitor asks, "—Is he a magistrate?" The novel is silent about Stephen's response or the motives of the questioner. One might wonder whether the student expects the boys to have magistrates as fathers, whether being a gentleman is meaningless, whether Stephen is somehow less adequate because his father, his first or biological author, is not a magistrate.

When he is sick in the infirmary, a boy tells a joke, but won't explain it. Stephen, confused, thinks back to this inquisition about his father. Instead of seeing his inability to understand the joke as an isolated and personal failure, Stephen sees it as a failure somehow linked to his father's inadequacy. Against the implied failure of his father to be a magistrate, Stephen's mind urges Simon's qualifications:

> He thought of his own father, of how he sang songs while his mother played and of how he always gave him a shilling when he asked for sixpence and he felt sorry for him that he was not a magistrate like the other boys' fathers. Then why was he sent to that place with them? But his father had told him that he would be no stranger there because his granduncle had presented an address to the liberator there fifty years before. (26)

Even before the first effort to query Stephen's paternity or authoring by the boys of Clongowes, the novel has identified Simon as author, a storyteller looking at him through a glass. Stephen's response to his parents in the first chapter is ambivalent. His mother (aside from her habit of crying during farewells) causes him fewer moments of anguish. The mother does not cry over Parnell—nor fight for that matter. The mother's occupation (unlike Simon's) cannot even implicitly be challenged as insufficient. The father, on the other hand, feels moved to justify the boy's placement in a school with his social superiors.

If Simon is a social liability for Stephen at Clongowes and throughout the novel, so too is his name. From Nasty Roche who demands, "—What kind of a name is that?" (9), to Davin who demands, "What with your name and your ideas . . . Are you Irish at all?" (202), his friends question and torment him with his patronym, the sign of his identity, and a sign bequeathed to him by a decidedly Irish father. Even Father Dolan must ask more than once to "hear" Stephen's last name. And yet Stephen, even at Clongowes, detaches himself from his father when he feels sorry for the father, not for himself. It is as though Stephen's sense of position is not defined by the father. Later in chapter 2, where his "equivocal position" (91) at Belvedere as a scholarship student grates on him, Stephen's sense is that he is not simply the product of Simon Dedalus.

Yet Stephen appears quite quickly to identify with his father and his father's chums, not with his mother. His recreational walks with his elders are male walks, not family walks; "the elders" Joyce writes of are clearly just men. That is part of what I mean by calling the book massively patriarchal. Women stand in shadows, important no doubt, but separate from the work of the world, or from the world of the fiction itself. Dante's debate over Parnell in the first chapter marks her as a peculiar female, a peculiarity noticed earlier when Stephen comments that she was a smart woman. Women exist in the novel as fantasies of men: the Virgin Mary to whom Stephen addresses his prayers in the third chapter; the prostitute who closes the second chapter; the woman on the beach in the fourth chapter who both suffers his gaze and then, almost immediately, is said to call to him with her eyes (171–72); the Emma whom Stephen imagines as his heavenly bride, as an erring female united to him by the Virgin (116); E. C. whose supposed interest in a priest grates on Stephen's pride in chapter 5 (220–21) and who, ultimately, for no reason to which the reader is privy, ends up as "the lure of the fallen seraphim" (217), Stephen's ultimate temptress in his villanelle. Within the plot, Stephen constructs these women out of the materials of his culture (literary and religious and social) and his own psychological needs. None of them exists separately with thoughts or needs of her own. None of them offers, as do Stephen's literary fathers, materials from which Stephen draws to construct his world. And none of them is a storyteller, the guardian of words and hence of reality.

The inadequacy of Simon Dedalus leads Stephen into literature and ultimately to the choice of literary fathers. We can see in the novel's juxtapositions potential causes for Stephen's choices. We are never told why he chooses to retreat into literature, but by looking at the events surrounding such retreats, we may infer cause. To do so is obviously dangerous in a novel that proposes that our lives have unexplained and unexplainable gaps in them. Yet what Joyce provides is juxtaposition, and our reading goes on making the meaning of the text.

THE FIRST CHOSEN FATHERS

In chapter 2 Stephen's personal and familial world abruptly changes; his family fortunes dwindle, and he moves from childhood into adolescence. Adding to those two disruptions of his life is a third: his father reports that Father Conmee had used Stephen's protest as a joke; Stephen was not a conquering hero as he had imagined at the end of chapter 1. At the opening of the second section of the second chapter, his family moves to dingier quarters; at the close of that section, Simon says all the Jesuits had laughed at Stephen's protest. Juxtaposed to these discoveries (rude shocks to his sense of self), Stephen's interest in romantic literature blossoms, seemingly acting as reassurance. Having read Dumas's *The Count of Monte Cristo*, Stephen acts out the part and imagines that, like the fortunes of Dumas's hero, his fortunes may change. He constructs a future transfiguration; a female that "without any overt act of his" would meet him in a secret tryst, and his adolescent "weakness and timidity and inexperience would fall from him in that magic moment" (65). The "strange unrest" in his blood, his "restless heart" (64), his dreams of Mercedes from *The Count of Monte Cristo*, and his longed-for transfiguration all promise an escape from home and an increasingly inadequate father.

Stephen's first movement into literature occurs in chapter 1 when he thinks of the stories of famous men with strange names in order to encourage himself to protest his pandying, or when he remembers "some great person whose head was in the books of history" (53), or the Romans who appealed their punishment and won. But this habit of turning to imaginative literature (whether history, fiction, or poetry) for solace accelerates in chapter 2. Joyce juxtaposes Stephen's first excursion in chapter 2 with a report of the family's financial decline: "In a vague way he understood that his father was in trouble and that this was the reason why he himself had not been sent back to Clongowes. . . . He returned to Mercedes" (64). In *Monte Cristo*, he discovers another proud, single, and maligned hero battling against odds to establish himself as wronged. In this identification, Stephen finds both hope in his social position and possible sexual satisfaction. Stephen's normal adolescent uncertainty seems exacerbated by the family's social situation, as the first section of chapter 2 ends with Stephen awaiting transfiguration through an encounter with "the unsubstantial image which his soul so constantly beheld," and the second section begins with another forced removal as the family slides down the socioeconomic scale. His father dreams of fighting his "enemies," with Stephen "enlisted for the fight" (65), but Stephen himself does not understand what he is to do, or how he is to fulfill the demands of his family. And rather than enlist in that nebulous fight, he increasingly moves away from the disappointing tactile world of his father and into the world of his imagination.

A Shelley quotation that ends the fourth section of chapter 2 is similarly juxtaposed with the inadequacy of his father. When Stephen travels to Cork with his father to sell the remaining family holdings there, the trip sharpens his sense of detachment from his father. He repeats his thoughts to himself: "—I am Stephen Dedalus. I am walking beside my father whose name is Simon Dedalus. We are in Cork, in Ireland. Cork is a city. Our room is in the Victoria Hotel. Victoria and Stephen and Simon. Simon and Stephen and Victoria. Names" (92). Even this litany means nothing to him; his life seems to detach itself from his current self. He feels "one humiliation" follows another (93), his father's behavior stands as simply that, humiliation for him:

> His childhood was dead or lost and with it his soul capable of simple joys, and he was drifting amid life like the barren shell of the moon.

Art thou pale for weariness
Of climbing heaven and gazing on the earth,
Wandering companionless . . .?
He repeated to himself the lines of Shelley's fragment. Its alternation of sad human ineffectualness with vast inhuman cycles of activity chilled him, and he forgot his own human and ineffectual grieving. (96)

Shelley's fragment (which contains five more lines) soothes Stephen because it provides fellowship for him; despite his sense of isolation, that imagined fellowship unifies him with others. The moon, in Shelley's verse, is a "chosen sister of the Spirit," a being that allows the spirit to find pity in its heart (the spirit "gazes" on the moon "till in thee it pities").[1] There are, of course, reasons that Stephen Dedalus finds in Shelley the resonance that soothes his despair: Shelley, too, in the nineteenth-century myth, stood isolated, despairing of his real world, heroic in his defiance of it. Like the moon in Shelley's fragment, Stephen stands at a great distance from his father and his friends; "an abyss of fortune or of temperament sundered him from them" and his mind "shone coldly on their strifes and happiness and regrets like a moon upon a younger earth" (95).

Again, Joyce breaks his texts with asterisks, closing one section. The fifth section begins with a brief attempt to right his family's fortunes by using his prize money as capital in a banking scheme. In his failure to have any effect, Stephen senses again "his own futile isolation." Unable to bridge "the restless shame and rancour" dividing him from his family, he feels that he stands "in the mystical kinship of fosterage, fosterchild and fosterbrother" to his family (98). He returns both to his secret sexual life and his wanderings. In his "image of Mercedes" he sees again "a tender premonition" of "the tryst" and "in spite of the horrible reality which lay between his hope of then and now," remembers "the holy encounter" he waits for (99). In short, the image of Mercedes comes to provide hope against the squalid realities of his life. His alternative seems to be sexual release. Within a page of this reference (the last in the novel) to Mercedes, he visits the red-light district of Dublin, there to find the first of his transformation scenes.

Paying attention to the words that create the scene for the reader, we can see that he envisions this encounter as a piece out of romantic fiction: the women are "leisurely and perfumed," the "yellow gas-flames" burn "as if before an altar"; groups are "arrayed as for some rite." He awakens "from a slumber of centuries." The whore who approaches him, dressed in a pink gown, takes him into a "warm and lightsome" room where "a huge doll . . . with her legs apart" decorates "the copious easy chair." The whore mimics his view of himself as a character in *Monte Cristo:* she undoes her gown, with "proud conscious movements of her perfumed head"; she embraces him "gaily and gravely" (100–1). He had imaginatively approached his Mercedes in a "moonlit garden," acting with "a sadly proud gesture of refusal" (63); the "softer languor" (99) of his Mercedes is mirrored in the leisurely ritual of the whores. Never has a visit to a brothel excited such romantic prose as Stephen's:

> His lips would not bend to kiss her. . . . In her arms he felt that he had suddenly become strong and fearless and sure of himself. . . . With a sudden movement she bowed his head and joined her lips to his and he read the meaning of her movements in her frank uplifted eyes. It was too much for him. He closed his eyes, surrendering himself to her, body and mind, conscious of nothing in the world but the dark pressure of her softly parting lips. They pressed upon his brain as upon his lips as though they were the vehicle of a vague speech; and between them he felt an unknown and timid pressure, darker than the swoon of sin, softer than sound or odour. (101)

To make oneself a character in a romantic novel is to choose a narrative father, a new author; to make oneself over as that father *might have done*. And that is what Stephen does. He takes his sense of *The Count of Monte Cristo* as a model of creator-creature relationship; he becomes imaginatively a creature of that literary creator, Dumas, just as he did when he acted out the part imaginatively earlier in the novel. Dumas's voice resonates to Stephen's emotional needs. Why Stephen needs to be other than the son of Simon Dedalus is implied in the plot:

Simon's fortunes in the world threaten to swamp Stephen. He turns to a literary father—Dumas or Shelley—because of the inadequacy of the "biological father," Simon Dedalus.

Fathers of the Faith:
Spiritual Fathers Lose, Triumph, Lose

Initially, Stephen accepts his spiritual fathers, the priests of the Church, without question. But even in chapter 1, their stature diminishes. Initially, in a scene discussed earlier, his father and Mr. Casey hammer on the failures of the priesthood that hounded Parnell to his grave. Later, Stephen wonders about their adequacy when he wonders what priests do when they sin (that is, when they are not—as they are supposed to be—perfect) (48). Immediately one does sin (Father Dolan in unfairly punishing Stephen). Such revelations of the limits of priestly goodness are, in part, mitigated by Father Conmee's ability to right the wrong, but Stephen will never entirely recover his uncertainty about these spiritual fathers. His uncertainty undergoes a period of remission following the retreat, as he responds to the literary art of Father Arnall who re-creates hell and its furies so vividly that Stephen imagines his own hell and repents.

In chapter 3, the father chosen is the father of the Church, and the father God, who both threaten and forgive. Stephen responds to them not only because of the power of Arnall's sermons, but also because his own tactile life is disappointing. At the end of chapter 2, Stephen feels his initial transfiguration achieved in sexual contact as a proud freeing of the self, but almost instantly in reading time sexuality becomes lust, imprisoning the self in one of Stephen's many labyrinths. His belly counsels him in the first paragraph. In the second, he imagines his evening, describing this new labyrinth: "He would follow a devious course up and down the streets [in the quarter of brothels], circling always nearer and nearer in a tremor of fear and joy" (102). After the first sermon (or what we read of it), Stephen contemplates his soul "fattening and congealing into a gross grease, plunging ever deeper in its dull fear into a sombre threatening dusk"; he sees his body "listless and dishonoured, gazing out of darkened eyes, helpless, perturbed and human for a bovine god to stare upon" (111). That bovine god echoes to the bull worship on Crete, rituals that focused on or in the labyrinth and to the Daedalian myth so important to this novel.[2] Stephen's sense of entrapment by his own action is clear. He even constructs the dogma of the Church as an imprisoning maze: "he found an arid pleasure in following up to the end the rigid lines of the doctrines of the church and penetrating into obscure silences only to hear and feel the more deeply his own condemnation" (106). When, finally, Stephen conjures up his own hell, it is not the overpopulated hell of the sermons where "bodies are heaped one upon another without even a glimpse of air" (120), it is an open field, populated only by fiendish "goatish creatures" (137) who circle to imprison him: "They moved in slow circles, circling closer and closer to enclose, to enclose, soft language issuing from their lips" (138).

It is this spiritual prison or labyrinth of language that the words and the Word of Father Arnall, Church, and God encourage him to see and to escape. The spiritual fathers, Arnall and the unnamed priest of the chapel, become—as Shelley and Dumas do in the second chapter—the progenitors of the newborn Stephen: he enters "another life" (146), is reborn into his faith. And that faith is only nominally the faith of Simon Dedalus who has, by this point in the novel, been utterly usurped by more "appropriate" fathers.

Even as we read these sermons and listen to the voice calling Stephen to repent, we may have doubts about this choice of father, of rebirth into another life. Arnall attempts, both in his language, and in the response he evokes from Stephen, to deny the maturity of our young artist. So, for instance, Arnall repeatedly refers to the boys as "my dear boys" (117), or "my dear little boys" (118), or "my dear little brothers in Christ" (108, 109, 111); Stephen sees himself and Emma in heaven as "always [the Virgin's] children" (116). Such a fatherhood proposes perpetual childhood for Stephen, perpetual submission to the views of others. It is no wonder that he finds these fathers inadequate in chapter 4; they would enforce sexual regression, limit his verbal and physical and spiritual freedom; they invite him into a world of "chill and order" (161). To choose a father who seems to advocate regression might spell an end to maturation. Christ demands that his followers become again like little children; hence Father Arnall's repeated association of the boys as his "little or dear little brothers." Sexually, Stephen's repentance causes him to revert to what he imagines to be prepubescent asexuality, purity. In that way, this choice of fathers is doomed (even before Freud told us that). And Stephen makes of the Church's dogma and ritual another labyrinth, this one a labyrinth designed not to imprison the Minotaur, but his own body and sexuality. In a way, then, the Church makes Stephen see himself as another hybrid. As the Minotaur is both human and bovine, so Stephen is soul and body. He rejects his body in chapter 3: "Who made it to be like that, a bestial part of the body able to understand bestially and desire bestially? . . . His soul sickened at the thought of a torpid snaky life feeding itslef [sic] out of the tender marrow of his life. . . ." (139–40). His real life is the life of the soul. So, in chapter 4, he devises the prison for his body, the works of faith and piety that will control (and do so) his sexuality, the "torpid snaky life." This prison, this father, too, must be escaped. It offers no liberation; he feels himself unable to love, and unable "to merge his life in the common tide of other lives" (151).

However much Stephen strives to imprison his sexual being, his purity and piety provide no freedom, no release. The last spiritual father with any power over Stephen offers him a priestly vocation. But the priests, the authors, the fathers who owned the Word in chapter 3 now possess the language of discredited authority; even before he rejects the priesthood, he feels that "their judgments . . . sounded a little childish . . . and had made him feel . . . as though he were slowly passing out of an accustomed world and were hearing its language for the last time" (156). The language with which his goatish devils encircled him is now the language of the Church, and that language and its voices, that system, proposes entrapment, threatening "to end for ever, in time and in eternity, his freedom" (161–62). This father won't do either; the authorial language is not right.

Storytellers and Patriarchy

The "New" "Old father, old artificer," Daedalus

Stephen's ultimate father appears most vividly in the novel after he has rejected the authorial language and voice of his spiritual fathers in a moment of epiphany on the beach. Stephen prepares for that moment by disengaging from earlier fathers and their voices. He has silently but irrevocably rejected a priestly vocation offered by the latest representative of his spiritual fathers; he has exiled himself from the Roman Catholic church; he has chosen to fall from grace, to deny the plot of his jesuitical fathers. "He would never swing the thurible before the tabernacle as priest"; "he would fall silently, in an instant" (162).

In this humor, having figuratively escaped the spiritual fathers of the Church, he literally escapes Simon, "walking rapidly lest his father's shrill whistle might call him back" (164). Choosing to go to university is constructed as an escape from false and repressive fathers, fathers who deny his need to mature: "he had passed beyond the challenge of the sentries who had stood as guardians of his boyhood and had sought to keep him among them that he might be subject to them and serve their ends." His destiny, "the end he had been born to serve yet did not see had led him to escape by an unseen path," "beckoned to him once more and a new adventure was about to be opened to him" (165). The author of that destiny is, like his path, as yet unseen.

Although much of his journey to his new adventure is imaged as an escape from fathers, a point made too unequivocally by Edmund Epstein,[3] Stephen's growing family of literary fathers aids him, marks the "unseen path." As he literally walks away from Simon and figuratively walks away from his religious fathers, he worries that his pride, his "dispassionate certitude" (166), will divide him from love and generosity. To escape these self-deprecating thoughts, he turns to literary fathers, drawing a "phrase from his treasure" hoard:

—A day of dappled seaborne clouds.
The phrase and the day and the scene harmonised in a chord. Words. Was it their colours? He allowed them to glow and fade,

hue after hue: sunrise gold, the russet and green of apple orchards, azure of waves, the greyfringed fleece of clouds. No, it was not their colours: it was the poise and balance of the period itself. (166)

Wondering at his love of the phrase he borrowed from Hugh Miller, he muses on how little he cares for language as a reflection of a shared world and speculates that he likes to contemplate in it "an inner world of individual emotions mirrored perfectly in a lucid supple periodic prose" (167). The scene is filled with literary ancestors. Cardinal Newman's "proud cadence" encapsulates his sense of "an elfin prelude" of freedom (165); Miller's phrase sparks his self-contemplation;[4] Rimbaud's "Voyelles," assigning colors to vowels, echoes as Stephen assigns colors to words.[5] Leaving two sets of fathers (Simon and Stephen's churchly fathers) seems to require a new set, one that Stephen constructs out of the literary culture of his time.

These literary fathers—and their words and voices—prepare the way for the central father, Daedalus. Stephen hears his classmates call to him, "Stephanos Dedalos" (168); he hears his destiny, an issue of some urgency given his rejection of other destinies. Joyce marks the urgency with the repeated "now."

> Now, as never before, his strange name seemed to him a prophecy. . . . Now, at the name of the fabulous artificer, he seemed to hear the noise of dim waves and to see a winged form flying above the waves and slowly climbing the air. . . . Was it a quaint device opening a page of some medieval book of prophecies and symbols, a hawklike man flying sunward above the sea, a prophecy of the end he had been born to serve and had been following through the mists of childhood and boyhood, a symbol of the artist forging anew in his workshop out of the sluggish matter of the earth a new soaring impalpable imperishable being? (168–69)

Stephen sees in the sign, his name, what he feels is signified, his destiny ("a symbol of the artist"). Daedalus, the master artisan who constructed a labyrinth on Crete to contain the Minotaur, and who was imprisoned within his own maze to protect its secrets, provides for our culture a type of the artist, used and mistreated by the powerful, but ultimately triumphant.

Joyce and his contemporaries had reasons for renewed interest in this ancient myth, as Jackson I. Cope has pointed out. In 1900, Sir Arthur Evans unearthed on Crete incontrovertible evidence of a labyrinth, of bull worship, and of ritual dancing in the labyrinth; researchers reported "'exquisite works of painting'" there. The figure of Daedalus emerged as fact, or at the least as "fabulous history."[6] While the excavations confirmed a land of art and ritual and a labyrinth, they merely added a grain of truth to the story of an artist and his son imprisoned by secular powers in his own art, the labyrinth. Daedalus constructs wings out of wax and feathers to escape, but Icarus, ignoring his father's advice, flies too close to the sun; his wings melt and he tumbles into the sea. The myth resonates to issues of art, of power, of arrogance and pride, of falling.

Stephen responds to this imagined call of what he hopes might be his destiny. The soul that had hung back from the director's call to priesthood assents: "Yes! Yes! Yes! He would create proudly out of the freedom and power of his soul, as the great artificer whose name he bore, a living thing, new and soaring and beautiful, impalpable, imperishable" (170).

Stephen's choice here provides some understanding of his sense of bloodline. If we take seriously Daedalus as the "Old father" of the last diary entry, we conclude that Stephen discovers identity through revelation of the father—as though this new father reveals Stephen's true genetic makeup; the young man sees, knows, his end, his telos suddenly; it manifests itself. In that sense, Stephen's experience on the beach fulfills his earlier expectations of destiny. And the fulfillment comes, as the expectations had, through words. As early as chapter 2, Stephen had imagined that learning words would somehow prepare him for that "great part" that "awaited him" in the world (62). And, now, at the point in his life when he chooses, he apprehends a word, a name called to him by his classmates, as the sign of his vocation to create, to be an artist. At this point in his life, he chooses or is chosen by a father who replaces his original father; he chooses to follow what he sees as a preordained vocation, that comes to him, unbidden, "without any overt act of his" (65), just as he had imagined it would come in chapter 2. The recognition scene of chapter 4, the discovery of his destiny in his name, leads directly to his vision of the girl on the beach, under whose eyes he "swoons" into transfiguration. But the male ancestor, the father who provides his name, Daedalus, demands recognition before such a tryst can occur.

How should we interpret Stephen's choice of a patriarch? While most versions of the Daedalus myth paint Icarus, the son, as doomed, constructing a tragedy for any young man who chooses Daedalus as father, the myth does not always speak with one voice. Another version of the tale paints Icarus as triumphant. Gabriele D'Annunzio's use of the myth in *Ditirambo IV* exalted Icarus as artist and denigrated Daedalus as "technician." In D'Annunzio's version Icarus's true allegiance to Helios (the sun) overwhelms his allegiance to his Daedalian father. This story, the story Cope brings to *Portrait,* constructs the Icarian fall as a fortunate fall, the fall crucial to genuine art,[7] just as Christian theologians have constructed the human fall of Eden as fortunate because it makes possible the redemption of Christ. Precisely how we are to take Stephen's Daedalian father, given differing versions of the myth, is not clear.

How we "read" the Daedalian image is further complicated in chapter 5. There, attempting to justify his lack of interest in Irish nationalism to his nationalistic friend, Davin, Stephen refers again to the Daedalian myth. "When the soul of a man is born in this country there are nets flung at it to hold it back from flight. You talk to me of nationality, language, religion. I shall try to fly by those nets" (203). Trapped in the labyrinth, Stephen sees his only hope as flight, departure, transcendence. Yet the sentence itself is ambiguous: to *fly by* may be to *fly by means of* as well as to *fly beyond,* and if Stephen is trapped in a labyrinth as his newfound father was, it may be that Stephen created the labyrinth just as Daedalus created his own. And finally, the ambiguity about Daedalus stems in part from Stephen's sense of sonship. If he is indeed the son of Daedalus, he may be destined not just to fall in the Catholic sense of a "fall from grace"; he may be destined to die as Icarus is in most versions of the myth, a possibility suggested by the cries of Stephen's classmate, "—O, cripes, I'm drownded" (169) in chapter 4.

We can resolve these ambiguities by choosing one discourse to bring to the text of *Portrait;* or we can (and this is my preference) recognize the text's inadequate information and refuse to resolve what seem to be mutually exclusive possibilities, instead holding them all together in our minds.

THE FATHERS OF ART

Chapter 4 ends with Stephen's triumphant choice of Daedalus as father, a choice that harbors negative as well as positive plots for the life Daedalus as author would write for a son. But Stephen's "family" is completed in chapter 5. There he chooses kinship with various authors of his culture. Words borrowed from Harold Bloom's *Anxiety of Influence,* if not his sense of literary history, can help us comprehend how the choice of literary "influences" or mentors is a choice about paternity. Bloom adopts Freudian terms to describe the relationship between what he calls "strong poets" and their predecessors. For him, the relationship mimics the "family romance" that Freud describes for birth families.[8] As the son wishes intensely for the affections of the mother, he imagines both the father's death and the father's animosity as punishment for his desire for the mother. By analogy, strong poets develop "anxieties" about their relationships to important and seminal predecessors. Yet the basis of oedipal conflict is not simple hatred, but also love and rivalry and competing need. Similarly, as Stephen requisitions the words of his literary ancestors he creates a family with rivalry and competing need as well. He uses these writers to establish himself as belonging—as he might belong in a Dumas novel or have written a Shelley poem—but chafes at the restraints that belonging entails. To go, as he finally does, to ill-defined kinsmen and to the mythic Daedalus, increasingly to borrow from literature without attribution, is to distance himself even from these chosen fathers. Thus, the references to Dumas and Shelley in chapter 2 are quite overt; the allusions to Yeats less overt or used to mark distance from Yeats; some allusions to literary fathers are distorted allusions; the parallels between his words and those of Swinburne and Pater and Wilde are unacknowledged in chapters 5 and 6. Choosing particular stories and their authors is a choice of substitute fathers.

Stephen's sense of vocation, his sense of his own identity as artist stem directly from that loose group of English writers we call "aesthetes"; Stephen's constructed paternity is directly visible in the materials he quotes and more massively visible in the metaphors he adopts for artistry. As Stephen adopts and echoes the special, talismanic words of these artistic fathers, Joyce indicates one of Stephen's paternal choices. Because these words were used in the late nineteenth and early twentieth century so often, they become signs or symbols of particular attitudes about art and the artist. To choose them, rather than other words, is to choose a kind of family of artists, a group that might be Stephen's kinsmen of the spirit.[9]

Let me take just one example. Stephen's designation of the artist as "a priest of eternal imagination, transmuting the daily bread of experience into the radiant body of everliving life" (221) positively reeks with the sacred words used by Oscar Wilde, Yeats, and Walter Pater to define the artist. Pater's character, Marius the Epicurean, had sought "to transmute [the very impress of life itself] into golden words"; Yeats admired and attempted to imitate alchemists because they "sought to fashion gold out of common metals merely as a part of a universal transmutation of all things into some divine and imperishable [another of Stephen's sacred words] substance"; Wilde labeled as art any "work in which the visible things of life are transmuted into artistic conventions."[10] Nor is the image of artist as priest unique to Stephen; Wilde had called Keats "the Priest of Beauty slain before his time"; Mallarmé was labeled by Symons as a "priest"; Yeats commended William Morris for knowing "towards the end . . . [that] he lived at a time when poets and artists have begun again to carry the burdens that priests and theologians took from them angrily some few hundred years ago." Yeats claimed in "The Theatre" that artists will become a "priesthood," spreading "their religion everywhere."[11] Yeats, who is directly alluded to in the fifth chapter, is perhaps the single most influential writer for Stephen Dedalus. I pause to quote one more comment of Yeats—one that begins to show how Stephen would associate the priesthood of art with nationalism, as he does when he hopes that his art will allow him to "cast his shadow over the imaginations" of Irish women "that they might breed a race less ignoble than their own" (238), or goes "to create the uncreated conscience of [his] race" (253).

In "Ireland and the Arts," Yeats told himself and other—presumably younger—artists what they had to do as *Irish* artists: "We who care deeply about the arts find ourselves the priesthood of an almost forgotten faith, and we must, I think, if we would win the people again, take upon ourselves the method and the fervour of a priesthood. We must be half humble and half proud."[12] Stephen believes that he is right "to try slowly and humbly and constantly to express . . . from the gross earth . . . an image of beauty" (207) that is art; simultaneously, his artistry is an act of pride, a decision not to serve (Lucifer's challenge to God) the forces of his world. In this combination of humility and pride, Stephen enacts Yeats's dictum, with "the method and the fervour of a priesthood."

Slightly more overt allusions reinforce our sense of Stephen's chosen fathers. As he conceives his villanelle, he mimics Yeats's theories about rhythm and poetic composition. Yeats urged that rhythm "prolong[s] the moment of contemplation, the moment when we are both asleep and awake, which is the one moment of creation,"[13] focused upon "those wavering, meditative, organic rhythms, which are the embodiment of the imagination, that neither desires nor hates, because it has done with time, and only wishes to gaze upon some reality, some beauty."[14] George Geckle argues persuasively that the time of the composition echoes Yeats's insistence upon creation "in the moments between sleeping and waking."[15] As Stephen begins his poem, "His mind was waking slowly to a tremulous morning knowledge, a morning inspiration"; as the world wakes up, he shrinks "from that life" and, feeling a "languorous weariness" pass over him, believes "soon he

71

would sleep" (217, 221, 222). At the same time, it is "the rhythmic movement of a villanelle" (217) that sustains his creation. When "The rhythm died out at once," he stammers, baffled: "The heart's cry was broken" (218). Similarly, Stephen's rejection of the temporal world so that he can gaze upon "some reality, some beauty" is clear. Later in the chapter when we read his aesthetic theory, we discover that he, like Yeats, believes that real beauty occurs when the mind neither hates nor desires, but is held static in the contemplation of beauty.

A third kind of allusion suggests both Stephen's allegiance to the writers that proposed the priesthood of art and his attempt to distance himself from them. He quotes a line from Thomas Nashe as *"Darkness falls from the air"* (232), realizes that he has misquoted the line *"Brightness falls from the air,"* and sees in that error "His mind bred vermin" (234). What is curious about Stephen's choice here is that this is the line Yeats quoted as representative of true symbolism in "The Symbolism of Poetry"; Stephen cannot even, initially, manage to refer to his artistic ancestors accurately. Late in the fifth chapter, he records in his diary that Yeats's "Michael Robartes remembers forgotten beauty and, when his arms wrap her round, he presses in his arms the loveliness which has long faded from the world. Not this. Not at all. I desire to press in my arms the loveliness which has not yet come into the world" (251). While Stephen labels himself, through his choices of metaphors and words, the child of Yeats's "last romantics," he sees his art as the future, as the beauty that has not yet come into the world. Taking from the word hoard of his culture, he looks to the future for vindication. Yet these metaphors carry with them the anxiety of influence that Bloom writes of; to move beyond these chosen fathers, just as to move beyond the rejected biological father, requires new terminology, that is, a new language. Stephen in his discussion of art recognizes that the chosen fathers cannot give him that language: "When we come to the phenomena of artistic conception, artistic gestation and artistic reproduction I require a new terminology and a new personal experience" (209).

At other points, he moves "beyond" artistic fathers by distorting their views. When he attempts to define the beautiful, he quotes with

approbation Aquinas's *"Pulcra sunt quae visa placent"* (186), and yet
he denies what is central to Aquinas—that all good is aligned with
God—when he defines the three qualities of art and the three stages
of aesthetic apprehension: *integritas* (wholeness), *consonantia* (harmony), and *claritas* (radiance):

> —The connotation of [*claritas*] . . . is rather vague. Aquinas
> uses a term which seems to be inexact. . . . It would lead you to
> believe that he had in mind symbolism or idealism, the supreme
> quality of beauty being a light from some other world, the idea of
> which the matter is but the shadow, the reality of which it is but the
> symbol. I thought he might mean that *claritas* is the artistic discov-
> ery and representation of the divine purpose in anything. . . . But
> that is literary talk. (212–13)

Whether Aquinas is just using "literary talk" or not, Aquinas does
refer directly to the manifestation of "divine purpose" as many commentators have pointed out. Hughes T. Bredin details, for instance,
how Aquinas identifies *claritas* with the Son, the Word, the "second
Person of the Trinity," or Christ.[16] Stephen's misreading of Aquinas
seems deliberate; all of his education mitigates against such a misun-
derstanding. Thus, as Stephen works out his own aesthetic, he appears
to distort Aquinas's ideas about God to serve his own purpose. In
another context altogether, T. S. Eliot claimed that true poets do
not borrow, they steal. And Stephen, despite his careful footnote to
Aquinas, appears to steal Aquinas's words and attribute to the philos-
opher-saint his own blasphemy, as he exalts art above the creator of
his childhood faith. Simultaneously, he not only chooses a metaphoric
father, but reshapes that father to his own purposes.

What these literary figures share is their ability to be manipu-
lated; even constructed fathers like Simon Dedalus behave in novels
as though they are consistent, probable beings. Literary fathers, the
constructed imaginative fathers of the text, allow authors and characters to draw from the intertext those words and ideas that resonate
most precisely with their desires and hence soothe their sense of isolation, rage, and despair. Stephen chooses Byron as the best poet, he

quotes Shelley, he echoes the Pre-Raphaelites, Pater, Yeats, Rimbaud, Hauptmann—all these mirror Stephen's sense of being isolated, above the dreary crowd of his contemporaries, able to see and know what mortals do not. Because these writers and their characters or personas frequently saw themselves as divided from other human beings but united with spirits of the ideal world, Stephen's choices unify as well as divide. He belongs, at least, to a select group of writers and spirits.

What the plot of *Portrait* suggests is that no son can be without some kind of father. Stephen does not kick free of Simon Dedalus and the clerical fathers of his youth to assume a state of singleness. For some readers, this fact represents Stephen's failure. For such commentators, fathers are biological, cultural, and political. They control sons, suppressing a son's individuality, forcing him to acquire an identity they approve of. Fathers, viewed in this light, prefer sons who remain subservient at least to the father's image of manhood; they may enforce perpetual childhood on sons who are not allowed the independence of adults. Rejecting such fathers and the *auctors* of a culture might permit a child to gain ascendance. For such commentators, the freedom and liberation from male authority is female. They assign the role of narration to the father, "desire" and freedom to the mother.[17] From such a point of view, Stephen is correct to reject the biological father and the repressing fathers of the Church, but wrong to adopt new fathers, new narrators or controlling forces.

Such a view appears to attack the political and psychological hegemony of the male, what we can call patriarchy. Yet it denies to the mother or to the female the human habit of narration. Insofar as we narrate to make sense of our world, to construct a causal explanation for the events of our lives, to deny that behavior to the mother is to deny humanity. Language and storytelling are male and patriarchal; being human is thus male and patriarchal. The desire attributed to the mother cannot be expressed, for the language acts requisite are denied her.

The self disconnected from parental figures appears to be the desired self in such a view. In a similar, older view, Edmund Epstein urges that Stephen's appearance in *Ulysses*, and his rejection there of

Bloom's offer to stay, support the idea that elder males always attempt to destroy the maturing, younger male. Epstein claims, "All the voices of his environment shout, 'Join me in my endeavors'; his soul says, 'You must isolate yourself.'"[18]

This view is neither one I am comfortable with (isolated selves seem to speak only to the self and not to living others) nor one that the works of Joyce, as I construct them, propose. Joyce's short stories and novels bemoan isolated selves; such beings stand trapped in paralysis from Eveline in *Dubliners* onward. Further, as I make sense of this novel, such a view ignores concerns central to Stephen's character. His repeated unhappiness stems from an inability to connect; when his mother prays that he will "learn what the heart is and what it feels," seeing Stephen as emotionally deficient, he responds, "Amen. So be it" (252). Stephen himself hopes that he will join others like him, who cry "we are your kinsmen" (252)—that is, he hopes for connectedness. And Stephen himself chooses voices out of literature and culture who urge him to "join in our endeavors," as Yeats had urged young artists to join his endeavors.

Harold Bloom has argued that all artists must in some way destroy the patriarchy—the elder writers—in order to create; they live with what he labels "the anxiety of influence." While that view seems to urge that isolation is necessary to the artist, Bloom comes closer to Stephen's view, however, when he quotes Nietzsche: "When one hasn't had a good father, it is necessary to invent one."[19] Stephen's adoption of various literary and spiritual fathers stems from the inadequacy of his "real" father and that need to "invent one." Repeatedly, these rejections and adoptions are mirrored in Stephen's sense of the *language* owned by the patriarch.

Framing the experience of the young artist is the displacement of the father, a transfer of allegiance from Simon Dedalus to Daedalus, the "Old father," the "old artificer" replacing his junior and inferior model. Should we wish to add to these framing fathers the epigraph (what Joyce quotes, from Ovid, is "And [Daedalus] turned his mind to obscure arts," a line followed by "and changes the laws of nature"), we might argue that Daedalus both begins and ends the novel and that

Simon is constructed as the usurper of the proper father. Whether or not we choose to start the novel with the epigraph, the constructed image of Daedalus—the architect of Crete's labyrinth, a type of the artist, the maker of waxen wings to escape his own artifice—authorizes Stephen's sense of vocation near the end of chapter 4. Without that *auctor* his destiny as artist would remain unwritten, the path to his destiny unseen. Patriarchy may be an evil, but for this young artist and for his creator it appears at worst a necessary evil. At best, it holds the promise of liberation, of finding a chosen people, a chosen fate, kinsmen. And to those kinsmen Stephen flies at the end of the novel, invoking the father, the patriarch he sees as crucial to his mode of life and art.

Chapter 7

FINDING A MODE OF LIFE: MONOMANIA AND ART

The protagonist in Joseph Conrad's *The Heart of Darkness* finds some comfort in his ability to choose his nightmare and to be loyal to the nightmare of his choice against the backdrop of corruption and despair. The fifth chapter of Joyce's *A Portrait of the Artist as a Young Man* seems to propose, slightly more positively, that the Irish select the monomania of their choice against the absurdity and despair of their world. Stephen chooses art; MacCann, universal peace and social betterment; Davin, Irish nationalism; Cranly, the conventions of filial piety. The chapter, most obviously, focuses upon Stephen's aesthetics, his poetry, and his escape. Those are the elements of his story, and this novel from first to last is the story of baby tuckoo. But, simultaneously, the chapter is the funniest in Joyce's novel, juxtaposing Stephen's monomania against that of other students and against the absurdity of Dublin as he knows it. Each monomaniac encounters resistance to his high seriousness; each fights against the absurdity, despair, and petty concerns of life; each finds himself isolated in, or makes himself isolated through, his loyalties and commitments; each feels out of sympathy with others.

Against the absurdity of poverty-stricken Dublin, Stephen Dedalus prepares for his artistic vows. He undergoes an intellectual process akin to that of a novitiate in a religious order. Like the fledgling priest, he attends school; in religious orders that school would be a "seminary," that is, a place of seeds and reproduction. Like the fledgling priest, he attempts to learn the dogma and mystery of his faith, a faith in the eternal imagination. Like the fledgling priest, he discovers that knowledge is not merely the movement of the spirit, but a discipline of the mind. All of these efforts are serious and sustained. Stephen's intellectual discussions of art occur, however, juxtaposed with normal and, at times, irreverent and rowdy university discussions. This counterpointing of aesthetic discussion and adolescent, raw comedy and of aesthetics with other loyalties and commitments both distinguishes Stephen from his compatriots and suggests that Stephen, like Mac-Cann, Temple, and Davin, is obsessed with his own concerns. That obsession marks him as adolescent. At the same time, Stephen occasionally participates in this humor. As artist, his life is fixed in the ordinary, and it is the ordinary that he wishes to transmute into the ever-living body of art. Paradoxically, Stephen's effort in this last chapter is to detach himself from all that binds the young artist to this mundane world: family, friends, school, nation, marketplace meanings of language, and ultimately his religious faith and his mother. To detach oneself from the mother is, of course, both an image of birth, as the fetus detaches from the womb, and an image—in the novel—of a final severing of that primary tie of life.

When Stephen urges his version of reality upon Lynch, he claims for it a privileged position: "We are right [to speak of art and beauty] . . . and the others are wrong" (206). The reality of Dublin is only that "gross earth or what it brings forth," even if it be the raw material of art. Out of that earth, claims Stephen, the artist expresses or presses "out again . . . an image of the beauty we have come to understand—that is art" (207). The comedy of the chapter conspires with the physical realities of Ireland to justify detachment from Ireland yet suggests the absurdity of the effort to be detached. For to detach oneself from the gross earth is to lose the raw materials of art.

In reading time we move almost instantly from Stephen arising from his rapturous sleep, almost postorgasmic in its tone at the end of chapter 4, to the squalor and absurdity of his family's home, fried bread crusts and pawn tickets littering the scene. Stephen demands to know how fast the clock is; his mother rights the clock to see how wrong it is and announces that it's an hour and twenty-five minutes off. Time is, indeed, out of joint for this artist, but the absurdity of the mother's actions suggests humor as well as serious commentary. That absurdity is followed by an almost slapstick routine of getting Stephen's washing water ready; he asks his mother; she details Katey to do it; Katey passes the job to Boody, who passes the job to Maggie. If filmed, we might expect to see increasingly young girls declining the privilege of playing Mary Magdalene to St. Stephen.

Joyce is not done with us; Stephen's mother washes him in a parody of biblical cleansing. His father's "earsplitting whistle" demands the sisters' attention. When one responds, Simon demands, "Is your lazy bitch of a brother gone out yet?" She lies, "Yes, father." Stephen points out both his father's error and, given his use of working-class slang, his father's new social status: "He has a curious idea of genders . . ." (175). Even the world Stephen enters as he exits this scene of familial absurdity is absurd: the voice of "a mad nun" screeches "in the nuns' madhouse beyond the wall" (175). Stephen's public and private context is so crazed that we cannot wonder why he wishes to escape that "gross earth or what it brings forth."

Entering the theater at his university, his potential seminary, Stephen appears initially to leave behind that absurdity. There he begins his first discussion of aesthetics with the proposition that "the beautiful is that which when seen pleases the eye" (he quotes the Latin, *"Pulcra sunt quae visa placent"*) (186). That is, like a good modernist, Stephen places beauty in the eye of the beholder. But such a formulation has obvious difficulties, for as Stephen points out, many things that please the sight do not necessarily please the "esthetic intellection" (186), which he assumes Aquinas refers to. Nor is it possible to know whether the words in aesthetic discussions are meant in their "marketplace" meaning or "according to the literary tradition" (188); indeed, Stephen's partner in the dialogue, the dean of studies, cannot consistently make such a distinction. The discussion with the dean, although it allows Stephen to introduce his major definitions, ends in his despair. The dean of studies frequently misunderstands; more crucially, his character and one of his misunderstandings remind Stephen that the dean's English, "so familiar and so foreign, will always be for me an acquired speech. I have not made or accepted its words. . . . My soul frets in the shadow of his language" (189). The university, too, is part of the grossness of the earth.

As though to reinforce that fact, the novel shifts into comedy. "Listening" to a science lecture, the students clown about F. W. Martino ("good old Fresh Water Martin"); Stephen demands paper from Moynihan with typical exaggeration, "—Give me some paper for God's sake"; and Moynihan irreverently responds, "—In case of necessity any layman or woman can do it," bandying about the Catholic teaching on baptism (191). Lecture material about "elliptical" and "ellipsoidal" evokes Moynihan's "—What price ellipsoidal balls! Chase me, ladies, I'm in the cavalry!" Stephen volunteers as a "subject for electrocution," and Moynihan, "seeing the professor bend over the coils," regresses into middle school and calls out, "Please, teacher! Please, teacher! This boy is after saying a bad word, teacher" (192–93). The teacher either does not hear these attempts at humor or, if he hears, ignores them (as any self-respecting teacher would). The students are, of course, just dicking around, with all the peculiarly male and adolescent connotations of that phrase.

Stephen both participates in this humor and detaches himself from it, worrying about his own response to Northern Irish speech: "—That thought is not mine. . . . It came from the comic Irishman in the bench behind" (193). Outside the lecture, Stephen speaks, with Cranly, pig Latin and argues about a petition for universal peace (refusing to sign). He does not, however, participate in the grossest humor, the young men's verbal abuse of each other. A student named Temple is everyone's favorite target. He lacks the wit of repartee, although some of what he says rings true and his behavior in the chapter occasionally parallels Stephen's. Temple, even more than Stephen, is an isolate. The epithets "flaming floundering fool!," "bloody ape," "flaming flaring bloody idiot," "flaming chamber pot," and "go-by-the-wall" are hurled at Temple in the space of two pages (200–1). Such crude wit abounds at the university. Moynihan is a "flaming bloody sugar"; Donovan "that yellow pancakeeating excrement"; Goggins "the flamingest dirty devil"; Temple back for his second dose of abuse is "a stinkpot" (195, 211, 230). Against this clatter of adolescent talk MacCann urges commitment to universal peace:

> MacCann began to speak with fluent energy of the Csar's rescript, of Stead, of general disarmament, arbitration in cases of international disputes, of the signs of the times, of the new humanity and the new gospel of life which would make it the business of the community to secure as cheaply as possible the greatest possible happiness of the greatest possible number. (196)

Stephen has no interest: "—The affair doesn't interest me in the least, said Stephen wearily" (197). The effect of the narrative point of view is to devalue MacCann's monomania, simply because it is presented so briefly. As readers we tend to identify with and focus on Stephen's response. Yet MacCann scores at least once when he attacks Stephen, "—Minor poets, I suppose, are above such trivial matters as universal peace" (197). Stephen asks to be left alone, just as he wishes his mother to leave him alone about religion and Davin to leave him alone about Irish nationalism. And when, later, Lynch demands a cigarette as payment for listening to Stephen's aesthetic obsessions, attentive readers may remember that Stephen asks MacCann, "—Will you pay me anything if I sign?" (196). MacCann's communal concerns contrast vividly with Stephen's solipsistic concerns. Concurrently, we might argue that MacCann concerns himself with the here and now, with life on earth, while Stephen seeks the eternal, relegating all mundane matters to the level of trivia.

As the scene shifts, we get another possible monomania, this one (from Stephen's point of view) even more provincial than MacCann's, Davin's Irish nationalism. Wedged between comic repartee, Davin urges his demands and the demands of his cause upon Stephen. Stephen announces his intention "to fly by" the "nets" of "nationality, language, [and] religion" (203), refusing to be the latest in a series of Irish martyrs. Davin's peasant mind allows him both to sign a petition for universal peace and to train for armed rebellion against the British, a contradiction paralleling Stephen's desire both to express himself and to use silence as one of his weapons.[1] For Davin, the only acceptable monomania is nationalism: "A man's country comes first. . . . You can be a poet or mystic after" (203). In one of the novel's most famous lines, Stephen retorts, "Ireland is the old sow that eats her farrow" (203). Against the monomania of MacCann for universal peace, and that of Davin for all things Irish, Stephen's own obsession reemerges: to be free of all constraints as the artist. His declaration of independence from international and national causes leads directly to the second sustained discussion of aesthetics.

He abruptly addresses Lynch, his second auditor, who initially seems no more willing in this discussion than was Stephen in the earlier ones:

> —Aristotle has not defined pity and terror. I have. I say . . .
> Lynch halted and said bluntly:
> —Stop! I won't listen! I am sick. I was out last night on a yellow drunk with Horan and Goggins.
> Stephen went on:
> —Pity is the feeling . . . . (204)

In short order Lynch responds as the artist as young man would wish, becoming engrossed in Stephen's belief that all proper art arrests the mind, suspends it, and raises it "above desire and loathing" (205), both kinetic emotions improper to art.

Yet even this discussion is interrupted. First, Lynch has apparently forgotten an earlier discussion during which the definition had been promulgated. He demands a repetition. Stephen retorts, "Do you remember the night? Cranly lost his temper and began to talk about Wicklow bacon." Lynch remembers the night all right: "I remember. . . . He told us about them flaming fat devils of pigs." Stephen replies, "you remember the pigs and forget [my definition]. You are a distressing pair, you and Cranly" (207). Lynch writes on the backsides of statues and ate cowdung as a child, both ironic corollaries to the serious subjects at hand—the first to aesthetic response and the second to the artist's use of the gross matter of the earth and "what it brings forth." He interrupts Stephen again: "—If I am to listen to your esthetic philosophy give me at least another cigarette. I don't care about it" (207).

Stephen reiterates the definition of beauty he'd given to the dean of studies, noting that different cultures recognize beauty in different valued features: "The Greek, the Turk, the Chinese, the Copt, the Hottentot . . . all admire a different type of female beauty" (208). Stephen dismisses the idea that we admire for biological function—"you admired the great flanks of Venus because you felt that she would bear you burly offspring" (209). For him, such views lead to "eugenics rather than to esthetic" (208). He prefers an Aquinian alternative: "all people who admire a beautiful object find in it certain relations that satisfy and coincide with the stages themselves of all esthetic apprehension" (209), *"Three things are needed for beauty, wholeness, harmony and radiance"* (212). Not content to define beauty as "Something we see and like" (208), he wants to find some catholic (universal) qualities. It is not surprising that a student trained by Jesuits would turn to the jolly friar as Lynch calls Aquinas.

If his auditor cannot remember earlier discussions and requires the bribe of a cigarette (as earlier Stephen had asked for money to support MacCann's peace petition), the rest of the world seems even less attentive to Stephen. He is interrupted by "a long dray laden with old iron . . . covering the end of [his] speech with the harsh roar of jangled and rattling metal" (209); he finds even the "crude grey light, mirrored in the sluggish water, and a smell of wet branches" warring against "the course of [his] thought" (207). And finally one of his schoolmates interrupts to report the results of final exams, mentioning by the way that "Goethe and Lessing . . . have written a lot on that subject" (211). Ireland and its denizens seem to conspire against Stephen's earnest theories.

Lynch, nonetheless, is the most apt auditor for Stephen's theories. He listens, queries respectfully, but does not challenge the theories Stephen expounds. And it is to Lynch that Stephen explains the role of the artist–God. Lyric, epic, and dramatic art differ in the relationship between artist, perceiver, and image, explains Stephen. When the dramatic mode is reached,

> the vitality which has flowed and eddied round each person fills every person with such vital force that he or she assumes a proper and intangible esthetic life. The personality of the artist, at first a cry or a cadence or a mood [the lyric form] and then a fluid and lambent narrative [epic form], finally refines itself out of existence, impersonalises itself, so to speak. The esthetic image in the dramatic form is life purified in and reprojected from the human imagination. The mystery of esthetic like that of material creation is accomplished. The artist, like the God of the creation, remains within or behind or beyond or above his handiwork, invisible, refined out of existence, indifferent, paring his fingernails. (215)

"—Trying to refine them also out of existence" (215), responds Lynch. Lynch follows this comic response with a more bitter one that exaggerates and trivializes Stephen's own view of Ireland's environment for the artist: "What do you mean . . . by prating about beauty and the imagination in this miserable Godforsaken island? No wonder the artist retired within or behind his handiwork after having perpetrated this country" (215).

Almost exactly in the middle of the fifth chapter and paralleling the Christmas dinner scene in the middle of the first chapter, Stephen conceives, gestates, and gives birth to his only poem of the novel, "The Villanelle of the Temptress." The poem in some ways summarizes the images of the novel, culminating concerns that have dogged Stephen since childhood. Images of the smoke that goes up from rim to rim recapitulate the incense smoke of the first chapter, the smoke of Uncle Charles's pipe in the second, the frail streams of incense of Stephen's prayers in the fourth chapter. The temptress herself fuses Eileen, the first temptress; E. C., the woman to whom it is addressed; the wading girl on the beach; the prostitute of the second chapter; and the Virgin Mary. It amalgamates spirit and body, art and sex, as Stephen's wet dream ushers in his poem, transmuting frustrated sexuality into art, the *"lure of the fallen seraphim."*

Stephen transmutes the materials of his life into a poem; whether that poem is an example of radiant ever-living life (his goal) is more debatable.[2] It is clear that the reality of E. C. disappears from the poem, just as earlier when he writes of the tram and E. C.'s invitation to kiss her, all human reality disappeared: "There remained no trace of the tram itself nor of the trammen nor of the horses: nor did he and she appear vividly" (70). Like the god of the creation, the artist disappears, "refined out of existence." The poem lays to rest, at least temporarily, the hold E. C. has on him, expunging his angst at her supposed betrayal of the young artist.

Stephen's final discussion with Cranly, focused on religion and maternal love, is introduced by another comic scene, and that ends focused on religion and the fate of unbaptized children. Temple first attempts what he sees as a serious discussion of lineage and "the law of heredity" (229–30). But, as usual, his comrades perceive his discussion as ludicrous. Cranly demands, "Are you drunk or what are you or what are you trying to say?" (231); other students egg him on, laughing at him as he announces himself and Cranly as "ballocks" (231); he discusses, with some seriousness, that ballocks is "the only English dual number" (231). Ultimately Temple attacks both the Church and his auditors for doctrines that consign unbaptized children to hell. He demands to know, "if Jesus suffered the children to come why does the church send them all to hell if they die unbaptised?" (236). He reveals that he is not, in Dixon's words, "quite orthodox on that point," when he asserts that the Church "is cruel like all old sinners" (236). When the other students insist that hell and limbo are to be distinguished, limbo being "like hell," "but with all the unpleasantness left out," Temple seems to sneer (236). O'Keeffe not only reveals his disapproval but his scorn when he urges that Temple be put "back into the perambulator" (237). On the point of limbo, "Ireland is united," claims Glynn, but Temple's last sally is that, in

Roscommon, "a notion like that" is called "—Neither my arse nor my elbow!" (237). This is the quality of the religious discussion against which we hear of Stephen's "loss of faith."

Temple is constructed as foolish: too earnest about too many things; unable to engage in the "wit" of his colleagues. And yet this scene of disparagement provides a foil to Stephen and Cranly's more seriously presented discussion of religion. Cranly's verbal constructs tie Stephen to Temple. Like Temple Stephen is an "excitable bloody man" (239). Just as Temple refuses to distinguish between hell and limbo, Stephen refuses to distinguish between heaven and "an eternity of bliss in the company of the dean of studies" (240). Stephen refuses to go to confession and receive the Eucharist during Eastertide and it is this refusal—an act that sets him outside the Church—that has created a severing fight with his mother. Cranly urges that Stephen think of his mother and receive Communion as a form, nothing more. But Stephen's mind "supersaturated," as Cranly claims, with his rejected faith, fears that acting out this blasphemy will set up a chemical reaction in his soul (240, 243).

Cranly's argument echoes Joyce's assertion to his brother that one of two truths in life was a mother's love for her child; Cranly urges such a view: "—Whatever else is unsure in this stinking dunghill of a world a mother's love is not" (241–42). Men have ideas: "Why, that bloody bleating goat Temple has ideas. MacCann has ideas too. Every jackass going the roads thinks he has ideas" (242). Temple has labeled himself a ballocks, but insists that Cranly is one as well. Every ballocks, every jackass has ideas; a mother has love. The appeal fails. Stephen refuses to "serve that in which I no longer believe whether it call itself my home, my fatherland or my church" (246–47), and he proclaims his path: "I will try to express myself in some mode of life or art as freely as I can and as wholly as I can, using for my defence the only arms I allow myself to use—silence, exile, and cunning" (247). Like Temple who is "a believer in the power of the mind" (198), Stephen will trust only to his own mind and imagination.

Stephen fights as a lightweight boxer, bobbing around the ring to avoid Cranly's heavy and direct argument that giving pain to an already pained mother is unnecessary, that love ought to outweigh intellectual uncertainties. In Cranly's dispute with Temple, the distinction between the two styles is dramatized as physical. Temple, hearing Cranly's "heavy boots . . . loudly charging," flees "through the dusk like a wild creature, nimble and fleetfooted" (237). Temple, like Stephen, attempts subtlety against Cranly's verbal crudity. Other similarities tie Temple with Stephen. He indicates his own Stephen-like appreciation of phrases when he wonders earlier if Stephen understands the "most profound sentence ever written. . . . Reproduction is the beginning of death" (231). And his interest in "the only English dual number" parallels Stephen's interest in words. In a world of contemporaries who have questioned Stephen's name and its Irishness, Temple indicates one feature of his peculiar relationship to Stephen by being the only comrade who insists upon Stephen's Irishness: "—I know all the history of your family too, Temple said, turning to Stephen" (230). Finally, while Stephen sees himself as Ireland's hope, wondering how he can shape Irish women so that they give birth to better human beings or asserting that he will "create the uncreated conscience of [his] race" (253), Cranly has ironically pointed to Temple in the earlier scene and said "with scorn to the others. Look at Ireland's hope!" (231). We ought not to dismiss Temple as quickly as Cranly seems to. That he is peculiar is obvious, but much of his peculiarity mimics Stephen's peculiarity.

Stephen's discussion with Cranly is punctuated by thoughts of exile as he determines that even his comrade, to whom he has confessed so often, will betray him, verbally abuse him as he has others, and eventually leave him. Throughout the chapter and most obviously here in Stephen's last sustained contact with a peer, Stephen constructs his escape as exile, a condition forced upon him by the Dublin that created him. Like Temple who flees "nimbly and like a wild creature" from Cranly's loud, rough boots, Stephen sees his need for flight using "silence [and] cunning." The chapter's picture of Dublin is overtly Stephen's; it is the gross matter he will transmute into ever-living life. His cause, his obsession, seems to offer transcendence, a flight to creatures like himself.

But if everyone else's cause appears at least slightly ludicrous, and if Dublin itself seems absurd, parallels between Stephen's behavior and that of his classmates can both increase our respect for the other students and allow us to see Stephen's responses as less special than he does. MacCann, Davin, and Temple, like Stephen, fight against the paralysis of Dublin; like Stephen, they endure mockery and betrayal by their friends; they too live in a world of absurdity. If life be absurd, as this chapter suggests, hoping to escape absurdity is hoping to escape life; to encounter reality for the millionth time is to encounter the absurdity of life as well as its beauty. The comedy in this chapter reinforces that sense of life, however much it may frustrate the seriousness of youth.

Chapter 8

TEXTURES OF INDETERMINACY: THE READER AS ACCOMPLICE

Stephen Dedalus assimilates the meaning of prayers to the Blessed Virgin by bringing his own discourse to the text, his own explanation and story to fill in the gaps of the liturgy: "Eileen had long thin cool white hands too because she was a girl. They were like ivory; only soft. That was the meaning of *Tower of Ivory*. . . . Her fair hair had streamed out behind her like gold in the sun. *Tower of Ivory. House of Gold.* By thinking of things you could understand them" (42–43). When we read this novel, all we have are the words we know—words of the novel and words of our culture. But words are never very certain means of communication; they are always interpreted, always modified by the receiver. Just as Stephen discovers *the* meaning of the liturgy, so we discover *the* meaning of this tale by thinking about it and its parts. In chapter 1 I suggested that words—and to whom we attribute the words of this novel—shape the reality we see. In chapter 2 I suggested that we do not always know how to process those words—indeed, that at times we cannot make out what the plot of the novel is or what causes what in the plot. Here, I'd like to focus on what seems a structural principle in the novel: the gaps that a reader must fill in. Part of the joy of reading Joyce's work is that he demands intellectual engagement—to understand it, you must think about it. Some of the gaps are, at least in part, filled in by attention to their context; some are apparently gaps in the knowledge of the narrative voice. Some of the gaps are gaps in our knowledge; some of the gaps are clearly marked with asterisks. Two major interpretative uncertainties conclude the novel: Stephen's diary and his flight. Let me take a few examples of the difficulties and joys such gaps create for the reader.

In chapter 1, some of Stephen's schoolmates are caught doing something. After a series of guesses by his classmates, Stephen is told that they were smugging. He—and the reader—are not certain what "smugging" is. Through a detective process and by following Stephen's associations, the reader determines that smugging is somehow sexual, specifically homosexual. Just after the Christmas dinner scene, and introduced only by asterisks that let us know time or place has changed, we hear first that "they were caught near the Hill of Lyons"; then Cecil Thunder tells us that the same "they" have "fecked cash out of the rector's room" (40). Stephen's thoughts respond, "But that was stealing. How could they have done that?" (40). Stephen clearly knows the slang word "fecked," and the narrative of the novel tells us both what the word means and that Stephen understands this discourse.

Cecil Thunder's analysis is rejected by Wells, who claims: "A fat lot you know about it. . . . I know why they scut." After some initial hesitance, Wells reveals the "truth": they drank the sacristy wine, "And that's why they ran away, if you want to know" (40). This possibility is clear to all—readers and listeners—and prompts Stephen's wondering about how anyone could go into such a "holy place" and do such an unthinkable act (40). But Athy rejoins, "You are all wrong" (41), and points to Simon Moonan as the man with the truth. And the truth is that "They were caught with Simon Moonan and Tusker Boyle in the square one night" (42). The listeners (and many readers) are baffled:

> The fellows looked at him and asked:
> —Caught?

—What doing?
Athy said:
—Smugging.
All the fellows were silent: and Athy said:
—And that's why. (42)

This is not so clear. The narrative does not clear up the confusion, at least not directly. Here are Stephen's musings:

> He wanted to ask somebody about it. What did that mean about the smugging in the square? Why did the five fellows out of the higher line run away for that? It was a joke, he thought. Simon Moonan had nice clothes. . . . And one day Boyle had said that an elephant had two tuskers instead of two tusks and that was why he was called Tusker Boyle but some fellows called him Lady Boyle because he was always at his nails, paring them.
> Eileen had long thin cool white hands too because she was a girl. . . . By thinking of things you could understand them.
> But why in the square? (42–43)

Stephen's reverie continues as he contemplates what people do in the square and attempts, by thinking about it, to understand it. He doesn't know even as much as we know; so, for instance, when he thinks about the graffiti on the wall, he sees only a sketch of a bearded man. Adult readers see a drawing of female genitalia: "a drawing in red pencil of a bearded man. . . . It had a funny face but was very like a man with a beard" (43). While the graffiti is a joke, he knows smugging is not all a joke, "because they had run away," and he "looked with the others in silence . . . and began to feel afraid" (43).

We are never told what smugging means partly because Stephen apparently does not know. But he intuits. His mental associations lead us to assume (correctly) that the boys have been engaged in some kind of homosexual activity. Stephen moves from Simon Moonan who has earlier been identified as "McGlade's suck" (11) to Tusker Boyle who resonates of feminity: he "was always at his nails, paring them." That association leads to Eileen whose nails connect her with Boyle and to Stephen's memory of temptation as Eileen "put her hand into his pocket" (43). Thus the boys' behavior parallels his prepubescent relationship to Eileen. Sexuality—adolescent style—is associated with the graffiti of the urinals. Gleeson is to flog one of the boys, Corrigan, but, claim Fleming and Thunder, he won't be flogged hard for "it's best of his [Gleeson's] play not to" (44). The position of Gleeson emerges for the reader: he is, or the boys suppose him to be, a pederast, interested in the boys with homosexual preferences, or perhaps interested in any boy at the school.

Stephen completes his intuitive understanding: "Mr Gleeson had round shiny cuffs and clean white wrists and fattish white hands and the nails of them were long and pointed. Perhaps he pared them too like Lady Boyle" (45). Stephen's own early sexuality, and perhaps even some masochistic tendencies, are both thrilled and terrified by the idea of the flogging: "And though he trembled with cold and fright to think of the cruel long nails and of the high whistling sound of the cane and of the chill you felt at the end of your shirt when you undressed yourself yet he felt a feeling of queer quiet pleasure inside him to think of the white fattish hands, clean and strong and gentle" (45).

The mystery of smuggling, thus, can be solved by looking carefully at Stephen's train of associations: the reader becomes the detective accomplice. It is possible that contemporary audiences would have known the word, and known its meaning. Slang dictionaries define it as our detective work proposes. But the novel itself does not make its meaning clear; Stephen's mind filters the information so that we know only what he knows and this particular mystery is quickly drowned out by another in Stephen's mind: his unfair pandying by Father Dolan.

There are places where the novel does not "solve" our reading problems. For instance, after Father Arnall's sermons have sufficiently terrified Stephen, he confesses to a strange priest in the Church Street chapel. Readers know that Stephen's chief sins, from his point of view anyway, are sins of "impurity" as he tells the priest. We know that he has visited prostitutes and we know that he has been masturbating with some regularity—the secret nighttime orgies are self-induced. The priest focuses on one sin in particular:

Textures of Indeterminacy: The Reader as Accomplice

—You are very young, my child, he said, and let me implore
of you to give up that sin. It is a terrible sin. It kills the body and it
kills the soul. It is the cause of many crimes and misfortunes. Give
it up, my child, for God's sake. It is dishonourable and unmanly.
You cannot know where that wretched habit will lead you or where
it will come against you. As long as you commit that sin, my poor
child, you will never be worth one farthing to God. Pray to our
mother Mary to help you. . . . You repent of all those sins. I am sure
you do. And you will promise God now that by His holy grace you
will never offend Him any more by that wicked sin. (144–45)

In the entire disquisition, the priest refers to sins (plural) only once;
he refers to one sin eleven times. The critical consensus is that the sin
that so distresses the old priest and Stephen is masturbation, not the
fornication or adultery Stephen has committed. Yet nothing in the text
seems to make that clear. It is true that popular opinion associated
masturbation with insanity and criminality, and yet we do not know
with certainty which sin the priest focuses on so ferociously.

More obvious gaps occur almost every time Joyce breaks his text
with asterisks. So, for instance, in chapter 2, Stephen's father retells a
story told him by Father Conmee. Conmee claims that he remembers
Stephen and the pandying incident well and that he had spoken with
Father Dolan at dinner about it: *"You better mind yourself, Father
Dolan, said I, or young Dedalus will send you up for twice nine"* (72);
Simon Dedalus repeats the punch line: *"—I told them all at dinner
about it and Father Dolan and I and all of us we had a hearty laugh
together over it. Ha! Ha!"* (72). The chapter breaks, with silence and
asterisks. What are we to make of that? Do we suppose, as many
critics do, that Conmee has in fact betrayed Stephen's appeal (another
instance of a Judas)? Do we suppose, as Stephen himself may have
done, that his previous triumph was false as well as ephemeral? Do
we, instead, suppose that Conmee has taken the appeal seriously,
found a way to protect Stephen and allow Dolan to save face? The
last is as possible as any other interpretation. The effect of Simon's
story on Stephen is never alluded to in *Portrait*. If it be fair to look
ahead, we see in *Ulysses* that Stephen remembers himself as the child

Conmee saved from pandies. Even that extratextual information does not tell us how Stephen regarded Conmee's story at the time, and his own growth may have led him to a more positive attitude about Conmee. In *Portrait*, the scene simply shifts to a Whitsuntide play at Belvedere.

If we look at that scene, and Stephen's part in it, we may make some inferences about his response. In that play his character is that of "a farcical pedagogue" (73), and the play itself concerns a father-son conflict, parallel to both Stephen's family conflict and a potential conflict with his Jesuit fathers. Further, Stephen "thought he saw a likeness between his father's mind and that of this smiling welldressed priest: and he was aware of some desecration of the priest's office . . ." (84) as he waits for his play to begin. We might put those pieces of text together and argue that his father's story of Conmee's "betrayal" generates Stephen's growing disengagement with the Jesuits, his increasing awareness that they are not morally perfect, in contrast with "the spotless decency of [the priest's] soutane" and "his spotless shoes" (84). But the two scenes may not be connected in that way; they may simply be discrete entities, or they may parallel earlier and later scenes in a different structural pattern.

Joyce's realism may simply be capturing the indeterminacy of existence. As an early reviewer said, "Episodes, sensations, dreams, emotions trivial or tragic succeed each other neither coherently nor incoherently; each is developed vividly for a moment, then fades away into the next. . . . Life is so."[1] We do not always know the causes of actions; we often do not know the motivations of ourselves or others; we see that we can attribute meaning and cause in more than one way. Traditionally, we expect novels to *show* us how to interpret them; we have thought that novels will, with attentive readings, add up, explain themselves. But this novel in particular (all novels to some extent) frustrates that expectation. The text of Joyce's novel demands that we become accomplices in the act of creation. The reward is a consciousness of how we make meaning, how we attribute motivation. Our experience mirrors Stephen's as he attempts to make meaningful his own experience. That is not to say that all interpretations of these gaps are equally persuasive; readers feel that some stories created to fill those gaps are more emotionally satisfying and account for more features of the story we share in Joyce's words. That is, some accomplices are more able to persuade others to participate in their creation, accepting their completion of Joyce's novel. Reasonable persons disagree about how to fill in the gaps, how to make sense of this novel.

As I shape Stephen's character, and come to know it, I see his treatment by Conmee as appropriate and kind. I also write a story that claims Stephen feels betrayed, that he uses Conmee's behavior as one piece of evidence in fashioning his own myth that he is betrayed by those who have authority over him. That Conmee helps him to a scholarship at a prestigious Jesuit school seems to me to indicate Conmee's positive, not mocking, response to the small boy. But other readers, more focused on the ways in which the Catholic church is repressive, see Conmee's behavior as another example of the institution's perfidy—a perfidy clear in the sermons designed to terrify small boys about their own maturation and sexuality, to repress the human instincts of children by threatening them in persuasive and terrifying ways. That story, too, seems to me to have merit, to explain Stephen's departure from the Church in positive and healthy ways.

Similar problems of interpretation occur between chapters, as each one ends on some kind of high moment for Stephen but each chapter begins with negative images that belie that earlier triumph. How do we create the transition, becoming Joyce's accomplices, for instance, between Stephen's liberation at the end of chapter 3 into a "simple and beautiful life" of truth and faith (146), and his enslavement at the beginning of chapter 4 in ritual and complicated acts of piety, acts labeled "works of supererogation" (147)? My words here suggest my answer; "enslavement" is my word, not Joyce's. Each reader participates, and each changes the story.

Perhaps the least explained section of *Portrait*, and the section that confuses readers the most, is the diary at the end of the novel. Even there, a variety of reading opportunities exists. Some items in Stephen's diary may seem clear if we attend to how words and motifs accumulate and build in the novel. For instance, Stephen writes in his diary of a conversation with Cranly over his refusal to take Communion during Eastertide—a refusal that sets him outside of the Roman Catholic church. He concludes that Cranly is John the Baptist:

> Hence Cranly's despair of soul: the child of exhausted loins. . . . Item: he eats chiefly belly bacon and dried figs. Read locusts and wild honey. Also, when thinking of him, saw always a stern severed head or deathmask as if outlined on a grey curtain or veronica. Decollation they call it in the fold. Puzzled for the moment by saint John at the Latin gate. What do I see? A decollated precursor trying to pick the lock. (248)

Much of this we can puzzle out with a bit of biblical knowledge, for Stephen has taken items out of Cranly's life and seen parallels to the biblical account of John the Baptist, including his parent's ages, his wanderings in the wilderness, and his beheading.

If Cranly is John the Baptist, then Stephen must see himself in some way as Christ. Understanding why Stephen identifies himself with Christ depends on our adding a variety of passages together, to catch the curve of Stephen's own emotion. Not only does his first name suggest a martyrdom (St. Stephen being the first Christian martyr), but his association of himself with Parnell is an association of saviors rejected by their own people: just as Parnell, in Stephen's own mythos, was betrayed by his own, and Christ was betrayed by his own people, so Stephen faces certain betrayal and martyrdom. The myth has roots in Stephen's mistreatment by Wells in the first chapter. When Stephen writes his villanelle, the act of creation makes him both male (the poet) and female, for "in the virgin womb of the imagination the word was made flesh" (217); the villanelle is conceived. He and his poetry are virgin births, born out of his own imagination. He transforms himself into his poem, just as he claims all great writers do: the dramatic artist "remains within or behind or beyond or above his handiwork" and disappears as a person, "invisible, refined out of existence" (215). Thus Stephen becomes Christ, or Antichrist, especially when we consider his statement to Cranly that he will not serve. It is only fitting, then, that this Christ should have a precursor, and Cranly receives the nod in the diary.

In larger terms, the diary itself invites interpretation and thought. Why, at the end of a third-person narrative, does Joyce introduce a first-person form with the diary? Edward Garnett complained that the book fell to pieces at the end; an early reviewer opined that the protagonist ends in insanity, as witnessed by the diary, a series of fragmentary records of Stephen's last days in Dublin.[2] Some concrete points can be made about this diary. First, the diary parodies and balances the opening section of the novel, which presents ideas and experiences without causal pattern or logical explanation or interpretation. Now at the end we return to the beginning, at least in that way. Like the opening, the diary appears to be without authorial intrusion, without a traditional narrator modifying Stephen's experience by explaining it. As they do with the opening, readers become Joyce's accomplices as they make sense by creating their own story for the diary. Second, a diary by its nature is not finished until one dies; one may quit writing in a diary, but the form does not dictate an ending until death. If Stephen is to go on to encounter for the millionth time the reality of experience, then the diary implies that the millionth encounter will have as its aftermath the millionth and first encounter. That is, the diary form insists on an open, not a closed, novel—one in which experience has no terminal point.

Third, if Stephen is to be an artist, and if an artist matures as his aesthetics imply, from lyric to epic to dramatic modes, then this diary may be a lyric mode. When Stephen defines that mode, he explains to Lynch: "The lyrical form is in fact the simplest verbal vesture of an instant of emotion, a rhythmical cry. . . . He who utters it is more conscious of the instant of emotion than of himself as feeling emotion" (214). Many of the diary entries have this quality. They are Stephen's lyrical cries, records of his dreams, his fears, his encounters with his friends. And they encourage us to look beyond what Stephen understands intellectually to the associations of his life that might explain them. As readers we need to move those cries from "immediate relation" to Stephen to "mediate relation" between Stephen and ourselves,

Stephen's definition of epical form. Again, we participate in the creation of the story that then comes to be, for us, Joyce's novel.

In the best discussion of the diary thus far, Michael Levenson urges exactly this kind of act—though for slightly different reasons. He deciphers parts of the diary by showing the "echoes of earlier passages, repetitions of key words, puns, verbal substitutions."[3] He takes, for instance, the entry of 5 April and connects it with Stephen's vision of the girl on the beach at the end of chapter 4. In his diary, Stephen writes: "Wild spring. Scudding clouds. O life! Dark stream of swirling bogwater on which appletrees have cast down their delicate flowers. Eyes of girls among leaves. Girls demure and romping. All fair or auburn: no dark ones. They blush better. Houp-la!" (250). At the end of chapter 4, Stephen used the word "wild" nine times to characterize his situation; "'scudding clouds,' calls to mind the phrase that arouses Stephen's artistic piety: 'A day of dappled seaborne clouds'"; Stephen's welcome to life—"O life!"—echoes not only his sense of life calling on the beach, but, I would add, repeated instances of new life throughout the novel.[4] And the girls who blush in the diary entry are a grosser and less romantic version of the fair-haired girl upon whose cheek the "faint flame trembled" (171). Levenson sees this as "the romantic euphoria on the bay [passing] into an almost jaded sensualism."[5] Another reader might take the same information and see Stephen's growing maturity—not jaded sensualism, but self-knowledge that his epiphany on the beach was inspired as much by sexual attraction as by some Platonic idea of beauty. The accomplice, not the text, has changed.

While Levenson's story, his explanation of how certain diary entries "recapitulate" the events and themes of the novel, makes meaning and sense of parts of the diary, our readings are not completed by his analysis. One can argue with or expand his story. He believes that Stephen's repeated announcements of departure—to Cranly (245), in the entries for 3 April (to Davin), for 16 April, for 17 April, and finally for 26 April (250, 251, 252)—"create a cadence that risks turning the promised culmination into an on-going sequence of culminations, with each trumping the one before until the spirit of revolt begins to languish"; the "reader who shares the ardor of 27 April must begin to suspect that 28 April will bring not exile, only more ardor."[6] Another reader may simply see normal delay before departure, the difficulty of escaping Ireland and Stephen's need to convince himself as well as others of his intention. That reader believes that 28 April will find Stephen on the ferry to Holyhead.

Nor has Levenson exhausted the diary entries. He does not comment upon the entries for 3 or 10 April. Those entries are different in kind as well: the first records a meeting between Davin, Simon Dedalus, and Stephen; the second records some kind of vision, which Stephen labels "Vague words for a vague emotion" (251) in the subsequent entry. The first is like many diary entries: at least on the surface a "mere" recording that advances the plot of Stephen's life. The second is a lyrical cry perhaps of some vague emotion felt by the character. Because this entry, and others like it, resemble or record James Joyce's early epiphanies, some readers understand the diary as Stephen's first step into art—that he creates this diary as the first step toward writing the novel we are just finishing.

For these readers, the crucial dates at the close of the novel, "Dublin 1904/Trieste 1914" (253), indicate that Stephen's exile to Europe marks the beginning of his journey to the narration of his own life, *A Portrait of the Artist as a Young Man*.[7] For other readers that notation is Joyce's—his indication of having started the novel in 1904 in Dublin and finishing it in 1914 in Trieste.

Each of these uncertainties in Joyce's text demand an active reader who will share in the shaping of the novel. As we shape our perceptions by selecting and weighing the elements of our tactile experience, and by associating them with other elements of that experience, as readers we select, focus, associate among the elements of our reading experience. Reading is, thus, a human and creative act, analogous to the act of writing in all contexts. The truism of our culture, that truth is contingent and elected, underlies the style and structure of the novel. Joyce makes us accomplices in his creation of this portrait.

Nowhere in the novel is that role for the reader more obvious than in the ultimate determination we make: is Stephen Dedalus an artist transcending the corruption of his world as he escapes to Paris or is he a would-be artist, doomed to fall like Icarus into the sea?

Chapter 9

STEPHEN'S "ESCAPE": TRANSCENDENCE OR FAILURE?

A novel that begins "Once upon a time" seems to require the ending "and they lived happily ever after." Fairy-tale openings seem to promise fairy-tale endings of triumph and contentment. When James Joyce was writing his last novel, *Finnegans Wake,* he wrote to a friend to discover how "you begin and end a fairy tale or a little story in Greek." Explaining his request he provides the Irish formulaic closure: "So they put on the kettle and they made tea and they lived happily ever after."[1] Fairy tales, as Bruno Bettelheim reminds us, are optimistic, while myth is pessimistic: "we can never live up fully to what the superego, as represented in myths by the gods, seems to require of us."[2] Similarly, the bildungsroman conventionally ends with a hero's maturation, after various threats from the external world, into a functional adult with appropriate moral code, vocation, and, often, life partner. The form of this novel, in its most general terms, leads us to expect the ending to be positive, a sign/symbol of Stephen's real growth and triumph. The words of the novel, at face value, propose much the same kind of reading, for Stephen charges out triumphantly to "encounter for the millionth time the reality of experience and to forge in the smithy of my soul the uncreated conscience of my race" (252–53).

Stephen's "Escape": Transcendence or Failure?

All the conventions and the hero's own words in his diary predict success. Why then do we debate whether Stephen succeeds, whether his exile is triumph or tragedy? Perhaps most directly for two reasons: because the Daedalian myth competes with the fairy tale convention and because of our visceral response to Stephen. Readers do not always like how Stephen treats his mother and E. C., or his long discourses on aesthetics, or his treatment of Lynch and Cranly. They distrust a novel that presents them with what some have called a prig as role model. And because we do not wish to make the author "wrong," we seek ways to align our sense of Stephen with the novel's sense of him, and look for signs within the novel that confirm that Stephen is not perfect.

If we begin with the novel's structure, we can see the difficulty in determining our answer to this crucial and final question. The five chapters of the novel have repetitive openings and closings. Chapter 1 ends with Stephen's triumph over Father Dolan. His classmates carry him in celebration, and when he escapes their hands, he feels "alone," "happy and free" (59). At the end of chapter 2, Stephen enters "another world"; he "had suddenly become strong and fearless and sure of himself"; he swoons into sexual ecstasy: "He closed his eyes, surrendering himself to her. . . . and between [her lips] he felt an unknown and timid pressure, darker than the swoon of sin" (100–1). At the end of the third chapter, he awakes to "Another life! A life of grace and virtue and happiness!" (146). After his vision of Daedalus and the girl on the beach, he cries out, "to greet the advent of the life that had cried to him," he experiences the "holy silence of his ecstasy," and finally "His soul was swooning into some new world" (172). In chapters 2–4 this moment is imaged as rebirth or awakening to another world, another life. At the end of each chapter Stephen feels liberated. In chapters 2–4 some kind of swooning or dreaming figures centrally in that liberation.

Each chapter also repeats a kind of plot. The end of each chapter proposes that Stephen has solved some central quandary. So, for instance, at the end of the first chapter, Stephen's ability to appeal successfully to Conmee solves the problem of Dolan's threat that he will come in tomorrow and tomorrow and tomorrow to see if "any lazy idle little loafer wants flogging" (51). Stephen's increasingly restless blood and brooding spirit of chapter 2 plague him until he discovers that what he has wanted was sex: "he wanted to sin with another of his kind" (99), he thinks; his solution lies in his visit to a prostitute. And his rebirth into another life after his confession of chapter 3 returns him from the bestial existence of the beginning of the chapter to a state of grace. The "call of life to his soul" of chapter 4 solves his quandary of what to do with his life. In fact, we could say that chapters 2–4 answer that question in an odd way: chapter 2 suggests that his destiny is physical being; chapter 3, spiritual being; chapter 4, an amalgamation of spirit and body in art.

Simultaneously, however, chapter openings juxtaposed with these triumphant endings seem to deflate our hero and readjust the reader's sense of Stephen's experiences. Uncle Charles's outhouse smoking in chapter 2 parallels the greasy dusk of chapter 3, which mirrors Stephen's greasy soul, which parallels the mechanical and spirit-killing piety that opens chapter 4. The difficulty, for anyone hoping that art is Stephen's ultimate solution, is that, after his discovery of a vocation, and his rebirth into that world of creation, the fifth chapter, like its predecessors, opens with such negative images of Stephen's life that we may distrust the triumph that precedes it: "He drained his third cup of watery tea to the dregs and set to chewing the crusts of fried bread that were scattered near him, staring into the dark pool of the jar" (174).

The images seem to suggest that Stephen is repetitively following a curve that peaks at the end of each chapter only to be plunged back into the mire of "realistic" Dublin. Perhaps the flight from Dublin can provide an escape from that mire; perhaps, as for Icarus, the flight has potential but the flyer hasn't. Other readers think of a spiral rather than a circle: the repetitions suggest similar conflicts in each chapter, but each chapter brings Stephen closer to an accurate perception of his destiny. So, for instance, the dependence upon Father Conmee's authoritarianism is a less satisfactory source of liberation than the dependence upon a prostitute and one's sexual being, which in turn is less satisfactory than the spiritual being that triumphs in chapter 3, which is less satisfactory than the combined spirit and flesh of chapter 4, and even that scene may propose a solution less satisfactory than Stephen's exile. In this logical shaping of the novel, Stephen achieves his liberation, having moved up the spiral to art and exile.

There is another way to think about the patterns of the novel. In each chapter Stephen adopts a particular way of organizing the world and his experience. In the subsequent chapter something happens, or he experiences something that makes that organization inadequate, and he reorganizes, restructures experience in another way, yet each chapter disrupts the pattern adopted at the end of the previous chapter. If that structure be true, the adoption of art at the end of the fourth chapter is inadequate and the exile will, inevitably, be disrupted, beyond the bounds of the novel. Just as the mechanistic piety of chapter 4 adumbrates its failure, so too the ecstasy of art withers into what some have seen as static and pedantic discussions, not spiritual and emotional liberation.

If the structure can as easily predict failure as success, some of the novel's motifs are uncertain guides as well. If Stephen be Icarus calling on father Daedalus, then he will not escape the labyrinth of his father's making. Just as Icarus, out of pride, flies too close to the sun, destroying his wings and causing his death, so by analogy Stephen may, through his own pride, fall, not fly. The novel certainly allows such a reading; Stephen is repeatedly constructed as proud. He arrogantly claims that in the service of his art and himself he does not fear eternal damnation: "I am not afraid to make a mistake, even a great mistake, a lifelong mistake and perhaps as long as eternity too" (247). And he tempts fate by echoing the words of Lucifer, words of prideful rebellion that send Lucifer falling into the pit of hell:

—I will not serve, answered Stephen.
—That remark was made before, Cranly said calmly.
—It is made behind now, said Stephen hotly. (239)

But the novel permits, encourages, other views of Stephen as well, views that suggest his decision may be right. Ireland may not be an adequate homeland for Stephen. He urges upon Davin a sense of the stultifying reality that is Ireland for him: "When the soul of a man is born in this country there are nets flung at it to hold it back from flight. You talk to me of nationality, language, religion. I shall try to fly by those nets" (203). Stephen Dedalus certainly appears to have escaped some institutions and some conditions that threaten his spirit and threaten his freedom.

One of those "nets," the Catholic religion, may be seen as repressive. It is difficult to read this novel and not feel that the Church, at least as Stephen experiences it, denies his freedom and normal maturation. The child who is unfairly punished by Father Dolan becomes the teenager whose growing sense of sexual maturity is labeled as so sinful that he cannot "be worth one farthing to God" (145) as long as he has a sexual being, who becomes the young adult whose need to experience life is constructed as a necessary fall: "He would fall" (162). He can either join the Jesuit order, a life of "chill and order" (161) and passionless power, or he can cease to be a Christian. (Stephen never contemplates the Protestant faith. When Cranly asks him if he has converted, he retorts, "—I said that I had lost the faith . . . , but not that I had lost selfrespect. What kind of liberation would that be to forsake an absurdity which is logical and coherent and to embrace one which is illogical and incoherent?" [243–44].) As Breon Mitchell points out, a traditional bildungsroman might well have ended with Stephen's renewed faith at the end of chapter 3; the novel would imply that Stephen joined the Jesuit order and lived a fulfilled and pious life, filled with the glorious faith.[3] Modern readers might not find that conclusion satisfying, but the pattern of a novel of development would have been fulfilled. Yet, as the novel continues beyond chapter 3, we focus more and more on the static and stultifying nature of the Church and on Stephen's faith—a faith that leaves him unable to feel, as Stephen's experience is constructed as mechanistic piety.

If escaping the Church and the religion of his family—one of his "nets"—is a positive sign of growth, is the escape from his nation similarly positive? Ireland's condition, witnessed to by the poverty of her Catholic students, who worry about jobs as they complete their de-

Stephen's "Escape": Transcendence or Failure?

grees, and by the extraordinary poverty of the Dedalus family, where children amuse themselves by picking lice off each other, may be a nation to be escaped. Yet Stephen feels, near the beginning of the chapter, "glad to find himself still in the midst of common lives, passing on his way amid the squalor and noise and sloth of the city fearlessly and with a light heart" (177). It is also clear that Stephen's college friends admire him. The peace protestors seek his signature; Davin seeks his complicity in the national movement; Lynch encourages his aesthetic discussions, providing a generally willing ear; Cranly seems genuinely to care about Stephen's familial and personal conflicts. Stephen, although he is called an "anti-social being" (177), has comrades. Whether he might have had a future in Ireland or not is less clear. While the Jesuits appear interested in his aesthetic discussions, they also appear unable to understand him. As Stephen proposes that he works "by the light of one or two ideas of Aristotle and Aquinas" and then uses a lamp metaphor (if it "smokes or smells I shall try to trim it. If it does not give light enough I shall sell it" [187]), the dean of studies misunderstands the metaphor and discusses another, famous lamp. Then, again, he misunderstands Stephen when he tries to distinguish between "marketplace" use of words and words used in particular contexts, using the word *detain* as an example:

> I remember a sentence of Newman's in which he says of the Blessed Virgin that she was detained in the full company of the saints. The use of the word in the marketplace is quite different. *I hope I am not detaining you.*
> —Not in the least, said the dean politely. (188)

Finally the same dean queries the word *tundish*, believing it an Irish word (a mistake Stephen corrects in his diary). All of these inabilities to understand what Stephen is talking about suggest that in Ireland there is not a ready audience for Stephen, at least among the authorities of the university and Stephen's present way of life. "Stephen, disheartened suddenly by the dean's firm dry tone, was silent" (190).

Nor do the politics of Ireland offer much. Stephen's sense that

Ireland is an old sow that eats her farrow, his belief that leading the Irish spells martyrdom for any "sincere and honourable man" has its roots in the downfall of Parnell. The nationalists of chapter 5 urge him to join the Gaelic League and learn his own language or to join Sinn Fein and fight for Irish independence. Yet Davin, their most attractive spokesman, is naive, as interested in athletics as in politics, and is unable to see any conflict between signing a petition for universal peace and training in secret for rebellion against the English. When Stephen looks at literary nationalism, he sees little potential. Thinking of the Irish legends recently rediscovered by Lady Gregory and W. B. Yeats, he claims "no individual mind had ever drawn out a line of beauty" from the "unwieldy tales that divided themselves as they moved down the cycles" (181). And he experiences the Dublin response to real art, a response reminiscent of Arnold's philistines. He remembers being at the Abbey Theatre for the opening of Yeats's *Countess Cathleen:*

> The catcalls and hisses and mocking cries ran in rude gusts round the hall from his scattered fellowstudents.
> —A libel on Ireland!
> —Made in Germany!
> —Blasphemy!
> —We never sold our faith!
> —No Irish woman ever did it!
> —We want no amateur atheists.
> —We want no budding buddhists. (226)

If the best and the brightest slander Yeats's art, bringing extraneous political considerations to the theater, Ireland is no place for an artist attempting to express himself as fully and honestly as he can. Ireland is constructed negatively by the words of the novel. Although Stephen's consciousness controls much of that construction, it is difficult to see the island nation as very hospitable to a would-be artist with no money.

Stephen's third net, language, has increasingly been associated with repressive authorities. In chapter 1, language belongs to Dante and the priests' pawns or to the shrill Parnellites (their language being labeled as against God and Church). In chapter 3, language belongs to the devils who circle to enclose him, "soft language issuing" from their mouths; in chapter 4, just as he begins to forsake his newly acquired faith, language belongs to the priests; in chapter 5, "heaps of dead language" confront him (179), the alien, conqueror's language, which he has not "made or accepted" chafes his soul. By chapter 5, the only language Stephen seems to find compatible is that of his own "revolt" or nonverbal language ("the language of memory ambered wines" [233]). Language, with its implicit association with culture, authors, and authorities, is a net because it ties each of us to our own culture.

If, then, the nets are real and really destructive, why are we not certain that Stephen's escape implies triumph? Because they are nets that define us as well as nets that enclose us. Stephen's language and his culture produced him, as he well knows. If he wishes a rebirth as someone not himself, he wishes for the unattainable. The fairy tale is not possible except as wish fulfillment. In *Ulysses,* Stephen Dedalus defines history as the nightmare from which he is trying to escape. That nightmare is inescapable; our personal history affects our future. Stephen is closer to the truth when he claims to Davin that "the shortest way to Tara was *via* Holyhead" (250)—that is, that exile may lead to Irish nationalism. Similarly, adopting the weapons of "silence, exile, and cunning" (247) may make Stephen Dedalus more Irish, more Catholic, more an English language speaker than staying in Dublin would.

If we turn to biography and Joyce's comments about the novel, we again find conflicting answers to the question of whether Stephen's escape is triumph or tragedy. Joyce insisted to Frank Budgen that people did not attend carefully enough to his title, especially the last four words: *as a Young Man.* Few human beings would wish to have their success in life judged by their position at age twenty; some, of course, would like to have achieved what they appeared to promise at twenty.

James Joyce shares with his protagonist schools, events, friends, even enemies. Almost everything within Joyce's novel is based upon his own life or the life of his brother. Joyce's own sexual experience is dated by his biographer from about the same age as Stephen's encounter with the prostitute; he, too, heard retreat sermons and went to a small chapel to confess; he, too, encountered a young girl wading on the beach and dated his awareness of artistry from that moment; he, too, developed aesthetic theories verbally to his friends and in notebooks. His father, like Simon Dedalus, lost a patronage job around the time of Parnell's fall and slid into poverty and drunkenness bemoaning the "murder" of his uncrowned king. James Joyce, like his character, left the Roman Catholic church but was never tempted by the "illogical absurdity" of Protestantism. Joyce left Ireland for exile in Trieste, Pola, Paris, and Zurich. Even the character's name has its biographical source: Joyce wrote the story "A Portrait of the Artist" and signed it Stephen Daedalus, as he did with his first stories for the *Irish Homestead*. Such analogues and identities have led readers to see Stephen as self-portrait; at least in part he is.

But Stephen is not simply James Joyce. Joyce was a successful athlete at Clongowes, not a terrified, weak boy. Stephen is represented as separate from the life of his campus in chapter 5. MacCann in the novel is modeled on Francis Skeffington with whom James Joyce published an essay after the two of them had been denied publication in the school paper. In the novel, MacCann appears unable to connect with Stephen; clearly in life Joyce and Skeffington connected. Furthermore, Stephen's development is much more stylized than Joyce's; items that might have disrupted the singleness of Stephen's development but formed part of Joyce's are not present. For instance, Joyce, but not Stephen, both contemplated and attempted medical school; Stephen is to be purely the artist. Joyce's early socialist tendencies are nowhere apparent in the activities of Stephen Dedalus; Joyce's singing—a central part of his life—appears only briefly in Stephen's fifth chapter.

The analogy between the martyred author—certainly an active neurosis in Joyce's own life—and Parnell receives heightening in the novel. In *Portrait,* Parnell dies before Simon Dedalus loses his job and while Stephen is at Clongowes. In life, John Joyce lost his job before the death of Parnell (though the events may be connected) and while James is at home, having been taken out of Clongowes when his father could not pay the bill. The Christmas dinner fight, which occurred in Joyce's life, thus cannot be a disruption of a child's sense of the perfection of home: the home, for James Joyce, was already disrupted. Indeed Hans Walter Gabler tells us that Joyce moved that central scene from chapter 2 to chapter 1 for fictional and artistic reasons, shaping life to make art.[4] Fiction makes cleaner, more formed patterns out of life than biography can hope to.

Joyce puts into the mouth of one of Stephen's antagonists, Cranly, his own view about women. Stanislaus Joyce, James's whetstone brother, records that he believed only in two kinds of love—the love of a mother for her child and of men for lies.[5] Against that argument, Stephen Dedalus fights in the novel. While Stephen Dedalus's aesthetic and artistic practice follows Yeats's early works with some care, Joyce differed from Yeats and Stephen in valuing the comic over the tragic art. By the time Joyce was writing *Portrait,* he had concluded that the Irish should adopt the strategies of Sinn Fein (a group to which Davin belongs) for economic independence and nonviolent resistance.[6] Although we have much biographical evidence that Joyce modeled Stephen on himself, he told Frank Budgen that he was no longer interested in Stephen when he was writing about him in *Ulysses* because Stephen had a shape that could not change.[7] He said the older man in the novel, Leopold Bloom, fascinated him more. Stephen cannot be said to be Joyce unless one wants to argue that Joyce himself felt dead-ended, unable to change or grow.

Even if Joyce was simply drawing a portrait of himself, he had in letters distanced himself from the attitudes of the young artist by the time he wrote the novel. He had also failed in his first exile, perhaps in part because he went off by himself. In chapter 5 of *Portrait,* Cranly worries that Stephen's isolation is the most negative aspect of his exile. He queries Stephen "—Alone, quite alone. You have no fear of that. And you know what that word means?" (247). Joyce's own successful exile began with his departure with Nora Barnacle from the North Wall of Dublin. Biography cannot solve the interpretative question I started with in this chapter: Is Stephen's exile a success story or a tale of failure?

The uncertainty of the novel's closure is the uncertainty of life.

While some lines of images predict success and some failure, what is crucial is that we do not know; it cannot be determined. And that uncertainty marks a kind of realism new to the tradition of the novel in 1916.

In fairness, I should state my position. I think Stephen is doomed. If, as psychologists from Freud on have proposed, the successful human being acquires two abilities, how to work and how to love, Stephen is not successful, for he has certainly not learned the second. His mother announces his failure five lines from the end of the novel, when "she prays now . . . that I may learn in my own life and away from home and friends what the heart is and what it feels" (252). That experience, the experience Stephen needs to succeed in human terms, has not occurred. This picture of the artist—like the God of creation, indifferent, paring his fingernails—is so strong an image of isolation that I am reminded of another Irish tale. In Synge's *Playboy of the Western World,* the young hero happy in his love feels sorry for God: "and I squeezing kisses on your puckered lips, till I'd feel a kind of pity for the Lord God is all ages sitting lonesome in his golden chair."[8] Perhaps the artist will adorn a golden chair, but I feel a kind of pity for that image of loneliness.

Stephen must escape Ireland, but his escape even from the young woman he clearly is attracted to involves the last in a series of literary repressions, and he knows it. She asks, as recorded in Stephen's diary, whether he was writing poetry. Stephen responds, "About whom? . . . This confused her more and I felt sorry and mean. Turned off that valve at once and opened the spiritual-heroic apparatus, invented and patented in all countries by Dante Alighieri" (252). In fact, the hope I feel for Stephen Dedalus as artist and successful human being is based solely on his ability, revealed in the fifth chapter and in the diary, to see himself as isolated, hurtful, inadequate. Life, to which Stephen sees himself going, contains the E. C.s of the world, contains the pious mothers unable to understand a son's apostasy, contains frail and limited comrades whose gross humor foils Stephen's earnest seriousness. The ways of mortal beauty and the experience of life for which he leaves the Jesuits—including the squalor and disorder of his father's house—are inescapable, for they define the human condition. Attempts to transcend the human condition are, in the world I construct, self-defeating. Paris may hold promise, but the phantasmal comrades Stephen thinks he goes to, the voices of his kinsmen are a fiction, the kind we invent when we need to escape the blood and mire of human veins. The Joyce and the Joyce novel I create as I read insist on that reality, along with the names of streets, schedules of trains, ads in the newspaper on a particular day in 1904—realistic details Joyce gathered for his second novel, *Ulysses.*[9]

NOTES

Chapter 1

1. Malcolm Brown, *The Politics of Irish Literature: From Thomas Davis to W. B. Yeats* (Seattle: University of Washington Press, 1972), 269.

2. David Krause, *Sean O'Casey: The Man and His Work* (New York: Macmillan, 1975), 4–5.

3. Nicholas Mansergh, *The Irish Question, 1840–1921: A Commentary on Anglo-Irish Relations and on Social and Political Forces in Ireland in the Age of Reform and Revolution*, 3d ed. (Toronto and Buffalo: University of Toronto Press, 1975), 259.

4. Edward Norman, *A History of Modern Ireland* (Coral Gables, Fla.: University of Miami Press, 1971), 12.

5. Ibid., 222–26.

6. Michael de L. Landon, *Erin and Britannia: The Historical Background to a Modern Tragedy* (Chicago: Nelson-Hall, 1981), 176. One practical reason for Irish loyalty to the Catholic church during the Renaissance—and so throughout history—was that the Protestant ministers spoke, almost exclusively, English, while indigenous priests of the Catholic church knew and spoke Gaelic. In 1600 and throughout the next two centuries, that language difference may have determined the religious sympathies of Gaelic Ireland.

7. Joel Mokyr, *Why Ireland Starved: A Quantitative and Analytical History of the Irish Economy, 1800–1850* (London: George Allen & Unwin), 16, 18.

8. Ibid., 10.

9. Ibid., 292.

10. Brown, *The Politics of Irish Literature*, 255.

11. Ibid., 350.

12. Hugh Kenner comments on this division in "Notes toward an Anatomy of 'Modernism,'" in *A Starchamber Quiry: A James Joyce Centennial Volume, 1882–1982*, ed. E. L. Epstein (New York and London: Methuen, 1982), 11–13.

13. Herbert Spenser, *The Study of Sociology* (London: H. S. King, 1873).

14. Émile Zola, *The Experimental Novel*, trans. Belle M. Sherman (New York: Haskell House, 1964).

15. Arthur Symons, *The Symbolist Movement in Literature* (London: W. Heinemann, 1899).

16. *A Portrait of the Artist as a Young Man*, Critical Edition, ed. Chester G. Anderson (New York: Viking, 1968), 203. Hereafter cited parenthetically in the text.

Chapter 2

1. *Letters of James Joyce*, ed. Stuart Gilbert and Richard Ellmann (New York: Viking Press, 1966), 2:134. Joyce was describing *Dubliners* in a letter to Grant Richards when he made the comment.

2. W. B. Yeats, "The Song of the Happy Shepherd," in *The Collected Poems of W. B. Yeats* (New York: Macmillan, 1956), 7–8. The poem appeared in Yeats's 1898 collection, *Crossways*.

Chapter 3

1. "A Reader's Report on *A Portrait of the Artist*," in *James Joyce: The Critical Heritage*, ed. Robert H. Deming (London and Henley: Routledge & Kegan Paul, 1970), 81–82. I have drawn all quotations of early views from Deming's collection simply because it is so widely available.

2. Richard Ellmann, *James Joyce*, rev. ed. (New York and Oxford: Oxford University Press, 1982), 405.

3. A. M., "A Sensitivist," *Manchester Guardian*, no. 22, 018 (2 March 1917); reprinted in Deming, *Critical Heritage*, 92.

4. Unsigned, "A Dyspeptic Portrait," *Freeman's Journal*, 7 April 1917; reprinted in Deming, *Critical Heritage*, 98.

5. Unsigned, *Irish Book Lover* 8, nos. 9–10 (April–May 1917); reprinted in Deming, *Critical Heritage*, 102.

6. John Quinn, "James Joyce, a New Novelist," *Vanity Fair* 8, no. 3 (May 1917); reprinted in Deming, *Critical Heritage*, 104.

7. Unsigned, "A Study in Garbage," *Everyman* (23 February 1917); reprinted in Deming, *Critical Heritage*, 85.

8. J. C. Squire, review, *New Statesman* 9 (14 April 1917); reprinted in Deming, *Critical Heritage*, 100.

9. H. G. Wells, "James Joyce," *Nation* 20 (24 February 1917); reprinted in Deming, *Critical Heritage*, 87.

Notes

10. Squire review, in Deming, *Critical Heritage,* 101.

11. A. Clutton-Brock, "Wild Youth," *Times Literary Supplement,* no. 789 (1 March 1917); reprinted in Deming, *Critical Heritage,* 89.

12. Unsigned, *Literary World* 83, no. 1 (1 March 1917); reprinted in Deming, *Critical Heritage,* 91.

13. Francis Hackett, "Green Sickness," *New Republic* 10, no. 122 (3 March 1917); reprinted in Deming, *Critical Heritage,* 95, 96.

14. Squire review, in Deming, *Critical Heritage,* 100.

15. John Macy, "James Joyce," *Dial* 62, no. 744 (14 June 1917); reprinted in Deming, *Critical Heritage,* 108; emphasis mine.

16. John F. Harris, "A Note on James Joyce," *To-Day* 3, no. 15 (May 1918); reprinted in Deming, *Critical Heritage,* 121.

17. Virginia Woolf, "Modern Novels," *Times Literary Supplement,* no. 899 (10 April 1919); reprinted in Deming, *Critical Heritage,* 125.

18. Harry Levin, *James Joyce: A Critical Introduction* (Norfolk, Conn.: New Directions, 1941).

19. Irene Hendry Chayes, "Joyce's Epiphanies," *Sewanee Review* 54 (July 1946): 1–19.

20. Hugh Kenner, *Dublin's Joyce* (Bloomington: Indiana University Press, 1956).

21. Wayne Booth, *The Rhetoric of Fiction* (Chicago: University of Chicago Press, 1961).

22. Robert Scholes, "Stephen Dedalus, Poet or Esthete?" *PMLA* 89 (September 1964): 484–89.

23. Richard Kain and Marvin Magalaner, *Joyce: The Man, the Work, the Reputation* (New York: New York University Press, 1952).

24. Kain and Magalaner, *Joyce: The Man,* 43.

25. Herbert Gorman, *James Joyce* (New York: Rinehart, 1939; rev. ed., 1948).

26. Ellmann, *James Joyce.*

27. Kevin Sullivan, *Joyce among the Jesuits* (New York: Columbia University Press, 1958), and J. Mitchell Morse, *The Sympathetic Alien: James Joyce and Catholicism* (New York: New York University Press, 1959).

28. William T. Noon, *Joyce and Aquinas* (New Haven, Conn.: Yale University Press, 1957).

29. John Francis Byrne, *Silent Years: An Autobiography with Memoirs of James Joyce and Our Ireland* (New York: Farrar, Straus and Young, 1953).

30. Padraic Colum and Mary Colum, *Our Friend James Joyce* (New York: Doubleday, 1958).

31. Leon Edel, *James Joyce: The Last Journey* (New York: Gotham Book Mart, 1947).

32. Constantine P. Curran, *James Joyce Remembered* (New York: Oxford University Press, 1968).

33. Robert Scholes and Richard Kain, *The Workshop of Daedalus: James Joyce and the Raw Materials for "A Portrait of the Artist as a Young Man"* (Evanston: Northwestern University Press, 1965).

34. Joseph Prescott, *Exploring James Joyce* (Carbondale: Southern Illinois University Press, 1964).

35. William York Tindall, *A Reader's Guide to James Joyce* (New York: Noonday Press, 1959).

36. Kain and Magalaner, *Joyce: The Man*, 111.

37. Thomas Connolly, ed., *Joyce's "Portrait": Criticisms and Critiques* (New York: Appleton-Century-Crofts, 1961); William Morris and Clifford Nault, eds., *Portraits of the Artist: A Casebook for James Joyce's "A Portrait"* (New York: Odyssey Press, 1962); William M. Schutte, ed., *Twentieth-Century Interpretations of "A Portrait of the Artist as a Young Man"* (Englewood Cliffs, N.J.: Prentice-Hall, 1968).

38. Robert S. Ryf, *A New Approach to Joyce: The "Portrait of the Artist" as a Guidebook* (Berkeley: University of California Press, 1964).

39. Marvin Magalaner, *Time of Apprenticeship* (New York: Abelard Schuman, 1959).

40. Homer Obed Brown, *James Joyce's Early Fiction: The Biography of a Form* (Cleveland: Case Western Reserve University Press, 1972).

41. Hans Walter Gabler, "The Seven Lost Years of *A Portrait of the Artist as a Young Man*," in *Approaches to Joyce's "Portrait": Ten Essays*, ed. Thomas F. Staley and Bernard Benstock (Pittsburgh: University of Pittsburgh Press, 1976), 25–60.

42. Edmund L. Epstein, *The Ordeal of Stephen Dedalus: The Conflict of Generations in James Joyce's "A Portrait of the Artist as a Young Man"* (Carbondale: Southern Illinois University Press, 1971).

43. Chester Anderson, "Baby Tuckoo: Joyce's 'Features of Infancy,'" in *Approaches to Joyce's "Portrait,"* ed. Staley and Benstock, 135–70.

44. Sheldon Brivic, *Joyce between Freud and Jung* (Port Washington, N.Y.: Kennikat Press, 1980).

45. Colin MacCabe, *James Joyce and the Revolution of the Word* (London and Basingstoke: Macmillan, 1979).

46. John Paul Riquelme, *Teller and Tale in Joyce's Fiction: Oscillating Perspectives* (Baltimore and London: Johns Hopkins University Press, 1983).

47. Phillip Herring, *Joyce's Uncertainty Principle* (Princeton, N.J.: Princeton University Press, 1987), xi, xii.

48. Bonnie Scott, *Joyce and Feminism* (Bloomington: Indiana University Press and Sussex: Harvester Press, 1984); Suzette Henke and Elaine Unkeless,

Notes

eds., *Women in Joyce* (Urbana, Chicago, and London: University of Illinois Press, 1982).

Chapter 4

1. Wells, "James Joyce," in Deming, *Critical Heritage,* 87.

2. Diego Angeli, "Un Romanzo di Gesuiti," *Il Marzocco* 22, no. 32 (12 August 1917); trans. James Joyce, *Egoist* 5, no. 2 (February 1918); reprinted in Deming, *Critical Heritage,* 115.

3. Wells, "James Joyce," in Deming, *Critical Heritage,* 88.

4. W. B. Yeats, "September 1913," in *Collected Poems,* 106.

5. Stanislaus Joyce, *My Brother's Keeper: James Joyce's Early Years* (New York: Viking Press, 1958), 91.

6. Angeli, "Un Romanzo," in Deming, *Critical Heritage,* 115.

Chapter 5

1. MacCabe, *The Revolution of the Word,* 16, 17.

2. Bernard Benstock in *James Joyce: The Undiscover'd Country* (Dublin: Gill and Macmillan, London: Macmillan, New York: Harper & Row and Barnes & Noble, 1977) reads the same scene and assumes that the "portrait of Stephen Dedalus is the charting of that long voyage down along the most difficult of roads in pursuit of the phantom moocow" (147). In my version of Joyce's novel, it is significant that the moocow moves while Stephen stands still ("there was a moocow coming down along the road").

3. Kenner, "Notes Toward an Anatomy of 'Modernism,'" in *Starchamber Quiry,* ed. Epstein, 24–26.

4. Bruno Bettelheim, *The Uses of Enchantment: The Meaning and Importance of Fairy Tales* (New York: Knopf, 1976), 24.

5. Ibid., 10.

6. Ibid., 25, 63.

7. Don Gifford, *Annotations for Joyce* (Berkeley: University of California Press, 1982), 133.

8. *Letters of James Joyce,* 3:212.

9. See particularly Anderson, "Baby Tuckoo: Joyce's 'Features of Infancy,'" in *Approaches,* ed. Staley and Benstock, 141–50.

10. Yeats, *Collected Poems,* 18–19; this poem appeared in Yeats's 1889 volume, *Crossways.*

11. Bettelheim, *Enchantment,* 24.

12. Gifford, *Annotations*, 133.

13. Mark Twain, *The Adventures of Huckleberry Finn* (Berkeley and Los Angeles: University of California Press, 1985), 1.

14. When James Joyce was a young man, he recorded incidents, dialogue, and images out of his own experiences. Borrowing ecclesiastical imagery, he called these records epiphanies, after the Feast of the Epiphany when Christ was made manifest to the wise men. By analogy, these were to Joyce moments when a spirit or a truth was manifest through the mundane world.

15. Epstein, *The Ordeal of Stephen Dedalus*, 34.

16. MacCabe, *The Revolution of the Word*, 56.

17. Yeats, "September 1913," in *Collected Poems*, 106.

18. Gabler, "The Seven Lost Years of *A Portrait of the Artist as a Young Man*," in *Approaches*, ed. Staley and Benstock, 35: "By the immediate juxtaposition of Stephen's dream of Parnell on his sickbed and the Christmas dinner controversy, Irish politics and the betrayal of Parnell become the chapter's organizing forces." Following Gabler's logic, we might note that Joyce reshapes his own experience here; his similar sickness did not coincide with the death of Parnell—indeed, he was no longer at Clongowes when Parnell died; he heightens Stephen's identification with Parnell by transforming the details of his life into a more "meaningful" whole for Stephen.

Chapter 6

1. Percy Bysshe Shelley, *The Complete Poems of Percy Bysshe Shelley*, ed. Roger Ingpen and Walter E. Peck (New York: Gordian Press, 1965), 59. The whole of "To the Moon" reads:

I

ART thou pale for weariness
Of climbing heaven, and gazing on the earth,
    Wandering companionless
Among the stars that have a different birth,—
And ever-changing, like a joyless eye
That finds no object worth its constancy?

II

Thou chosen sister of the Spirit,
That gazes on thee till in thee it pities.

Notes

2. Daedalus, to whom I return later, was a renowned craftsman who created a wooden cow so that Pasiphae, the Queen of Crete, could satisfy her lust for a bull. By order of King Minos of Crete Daedalus constructed a labyrinth to contain the hybrid offspring of this union, the Minotaur; Daedalus and his son were imprisoned in the labyrinth; in order to escape, Daedalus constructed wings of feathers and wax. Unfortunately, Icarus in the pride of youth rejected his father's advice to fly low out of the labyrinth and the sun's beams melted the wax. While Daedalus escaped, Icarus fell into the sea to his death.

3. Epstein, *The Ordeal of Stephen Dedalus*, 78–153, passim.

4. James S. Atherton supplies the identification in *A Portrait of the Artist as a Young Man*, ed. with introduction and notes by J. S. Atherton (London: Heinemann, 1964), 249.

5. Even here, however, Stephen seems to go beyond the literary father. Phillip Herring points out that in "gauging the appeal of words to rhythms to be greater than word hues, Stephen strains the bonds of apprenticeship" (*Joyce's Uncertainty Principle*, 152–53).

6. Jackson I. Cope, *Joyce's Cities: Archeologies of the Soul* (Baltimore and London: Johns Hopkins Press, 1981), 48–49. Joyce first used the name Daedalus to sign the ur-*Portrait*, an essay he submitted to the *Irish Homestead;* the *Fortnightly Review* published, in 1900, not only Joyce's "Ibsen's New Drama," but also a report on Evans's findings. It is almost certain that Joyce knew of the excavation.

7. Ibid., 49–51.

8. Harold Bloom, *The Anxiety of Influence: A Theory of Poetry* (New York: Oxford University Press, 1973), 5–8.

9. I have urged this view of Stephen in *The Aesthetics of Dedalus and Bloom* (Lewisburg, Pa.: Bucknell University Press, London and Toronto: Associated University Presses, 1984).

10. Walter Horatio Pater, *Marius the Epicurean* (London: Dent, 1934), 103; W. B. Yeats, *"Rosa Alchemica,"* in *Mythologies* (New York: Macmillan, Collier Books, 1969), 267; Oscar Wilde, "The Decay of Lying," *The Complete Works*, 12 vols. (Garden City, N.Y.: Doubleday, 1923), 5:31.

11. Wilde, "The Tomb of Keats," 12:304; Arthur Symons, *The Symbolist Movement in Literature*, 122; Yeats, "Happiest of Poets," in *Essays and Introductions* (New York: Macmillan, Collier Books, 1959), 64; Yeats, *Essays and Introductions*, 168.

12. Yeats, "Ireland and the Arts," *Essays and Introductions*, 203.

13. Yeats, "The Symbolism of Poetry," *Essays and Introductions*, 159.

14. Ibid., 163.

15. See George Geckle, "Stephen Dedalus and W. B. Yeats: The Making of the Villanelle," *Modern Fiction Studies* 15 (1969): 87–96.

16. Hughes T. Bredin, "Applied Aquinas: James Joyce's Aesthetics," *Eire-Ireland* 3 (1968): 61–78.

17. Colin MacCabe argues: "In so far as the text refuses narrative and the father, it can investigate the world of the mother that lies buried in a patriarchal society, but in so far as the text figures an omnipotent father [including the 'mythical father,' Daedalus], in so far as it still tells a story then women will figure as bagatelles, mere means of exchange between men" (*The Revolution of the Word*, 66). I fear that this view has the effect of effacing women, "the world of the mother," from the world of human beings, thus making it even more overtly anti-female than Stephen's view!

18. Epstein, *The Ordeal of Stephen Dedalus*, 5.

19. Bloom, *The Anxiety of Influence*, 56.

Chapter 7

1. Stephen says to Cranly: "I will try to express myself in some mode of life or art as freely as I can and as wholly as I can, using for my defence the only arms I allow myself to use—silence, exile, and cunning" (247).

2. A variety of views of the villanelle are offered in the following: Scholes, "Stephen Dedalus: Poet or Esthete?"; Geckle, "Stephen Dedalus and W. B. Yeats: The Making of the Villanelle"; Charles Rossman, "Stephen Dedalus's Villanelle," *James Joyce Quarterly* 12 (1975): 281–93; Bernard Benstock, "The Temptation of St. Stephen: A View of the Villanelle," *James Joyce Quarterly* 14 (1976): 31–34; Zack Bowen, "Stephen's Villanelle: Antecedents, Manifestations, and Aftermath," *Modern British Literature* 5 (1980): 63–67.

Chapter 8

1. Macy, "James Joyce," in Deming, *Critical Heritage*, 108.

2. Edward Garnett, "Reader's Report," in Deming, *Critical Heritage*, 81; "A Study in Garbage," in Deming, *Critical Heritage*, 85.

3. Michael Levenson, "Stephen's Diary in Joyce's *Portrait*—the Shape of a Life," *ELH* 52 (1985): 1026.

4. Ibid., 1025.

5. Ibid., 1027.

6. Ibid., 1020.

7. See, for instance, Riquelme's *Teller and Tale in Joyce's Fiction: Oscillating Perspectives*, especially 58–64.

Notes

Chapter 9

1. *Letters of James Joyce*, 1:400.

2. Bettelheim, *Enchantment*, 37.

3. Breon Mitchell, "*A Portrait* and the *Bildungsroman* Tradition," in *Approaches*, ed. Staley and Benstock, 73.

4. Hans Walter Gabler, "The Christmas Dinner Scene, Parnell's Death, and the Genesis of *A Portrait of the Artist as a Young Man*," *James Joyce Quarterly* 13 (1975): 27–38; "The Seven Lost Years of *A Portrait*," in *Approaches*, ed. Staley and Benstock, 25–60.

5. Stanislaus Joyce, *My Brother's Keeper*, 91: "He declared bitterly that he believed in only two things, a mother's love for her child and a man's love of lies—of lies of all possible kinds—and he was determined that his spiritual experience should not be a make-believe."

6. Richard Ellmann, *James Joyce*, 257.

7. Frank Budgen, *James Joyce and the Making of "Ulysses"* (Bloomington: Indiana University Press, 1934), 105.

8. John Synge, *The Playboy of the Western World* (New York: Modern Library, 1935), 64.

9. Writing *Ulysses*, Joyce sent constant requests for newspapers, maps, details from Dublin. He wrote his aunt, Josephine Murray (Mrs. William), twice in 1920 for "information about the Star of the Sea Church, has it ivy on its seafront, are there trees in Leahy's terrace at the side or near, if so, what, are there steps leading down to the beach?" (*Letters*, 1:136; see also an earlier letter, 1:135); the details are used in the "Nausicca" chapter of the novel. At another time, Joyce needed assurance that a man of normal stature could drop down to the English-basement door at 7 Eccles Street, as Leopold Bloom does late in the novel (and as John Byrne had done in real life). Such realistic details pervade Joyce's novel.

BIBLIOGRAPHY

Primary Works

Chamber Music. London: Elkin Mathews, 1907. New York: Huebsch, 1918. Edited by William York Tindall, New York: Columbia University Press, 1954.

Collected Poems. New York: Black Sun Press, 1939; Huebsch, 1918; Viking Press, 1937, 1957.

Critical Writings of James Joyce. Edited by Ellsworth Mason and Richard Ellmann. New York: Viking Press, 1959.

Dubliners. London: Grant Richards, 1914; Jonathan Cape, 1954. New York: Huebsch, 1916. Edited by Robert Scholes, New York: Viking Press, 1967. Critical Edition edited by Robert Scholes and A. Walton Litz, New York: Viking Press, 1969.

Epiphanies. Introduction and notes by O. A. Silverman. Lockwood Memorial Library. Buffalo, N.Y.: University of Buffalo, 1960.

Exiles. London: Grant Richards; New York: Huebsch, 1918. A play in three acts, including hitherto unpublished notes by the author, discovered after his death, and an introduction by Padraic Colum, New York: Viking Press; Harmondsworth, England: Penguin, 1951.

Finnegans Wake. New York: Viking Press; London: Faber and Faber, 1939. Corrected edition, New York: Viking Press, 1958.

Giacomo Joyce. Edited by Richard Ellmann. New York: Viking Press, 1968.

Letters of James Joyce. Vol. 1. Edited by Stuart Gilbert. New York: Viking Press, 1957; reissued with corrections, 1966. Vols. 2 and 3. Edited by Richard Ellmann. New York: Viking Press, 1966.

Pomes Penyeach. Paris: Shakespeare and Company, 1927. Princeton, N.J.: Sylvia Beach, 1931. London: Harmsworth, 1932.

A Portrait of the Artist as a Young Man. New York: Huebsch, 1916. London: Egoist, 1917; Jonathan Cape, 1956. Edited by Chester G. Anderson and Richard Ellmann, New York: Viking Press, 1964, 1968.

Bibliography

Stephen Hero. Edited by Theodore Spencer. Norfolk, Conn.: New Directions, 1944. Rev. ed. edited by John J. Slocum and Herbert Cahoon, Norfolk, Conn.: New Directions, 1959.

Ulysses. Paris: Shakespeare and Company; London: Egoist, 1922. New York: Random House, 1934, 1961. London: Bodley Head, 1937, 1960. Corrected edition, edited by Hans Walter Gabler, New York and London: Penguin Books, Garland, and Bodley Head, 1984, 1986.

Secondary Works

Books

Anderson, Chester. *James Joyce and His World.* London: Thames and Hudson, 1967. Photographs of Joyce, Dublin, Trieste, Paris, and Zurich; commentary on Joyce's life and acquaintances.

Bowen, Zack. *Musical Allusions in the Works of James Joyce: Early Poetry through "Ulysses."* Albany: State University of New York Press, 1974. Critical essays on Joyce's use of music; remarks on each musical allusion.

———, and James F. Carens, eds. *A Companion to Joyce Studies.* Westport, Conn., and London: Greenwood Press, 1984.

Brivic, Sheldon. *Joyce between Freud and Jung.* Port Washington, N.Y.: Kennikat Press, 1980. Section on *Portrait* is a Freudian reading both of Joyce and of Stephen, especially concerned with oedipal parallels.

Brown, Homer Obed. *James Joyce's Early Fiction: The Biography of a Form.* Cleveland: Case Western Reserve University Press, 1972. Discusses the evolution of Joyce's artistic techniques and his attitudes about Dublin and his characters from "The Sisters" to *Portrait.*

Byrne, John Francis. *The Silent Years: An Autobiography with Memoirs of James Joyce and Our Ireland.* New York: Farrar, Straus and Young, 1953. Byrne serves as Joyce's model for Cranly in *Portrait.*

Connolly, Thomas, ed. *Joyce's "Portrait": Criticisms and Critiques.* New York: Appleton-Century-Crofts, 1962. Collects nineteen previously published essays; good collection of critical opinion through 1962.

Deming, Robert H., ed. *James Joyce: The Critical Heritage.* London: Routledge and Kegan Paul; New York: Critical Heritage Series, 1970. Collects, in two volumes, early commentary on Joyce's writings.

Ellmann, Richard. *James Joyce.* Rev. ed. New York: Oxford University Press, 1982. The single most complete and accurate biography of James Joyce.

Epstein, Edmund L. *The Ordeal of Stephen Dedalus: The Conflict of Generations in James Joyce's "A Portrait of the Artist as a Young Man."*

Carbondale: Southern Illinois University Press, 1971. Essentially Freudian reading of Joyce, focused on Stephen Dedalus's need to mature beyond and escape the father in order to create in his own fatherhood.

Gifford, Don. *Joyce Annotated: Notes for "Dubliners" and "A Portrait of the Artist as a Young Man."* Berkeley: University of California Press, 1982. Line-by-line annotations of information readers may want/need about allusions, place-names, historical figures, etc., in *Portrait*.

Hancock, Leslie. *Word Index to James Joyce's "A Portrait of the Artist as a Young Man."* Carbondale: Southern Illinois University Press, 1967. Useful reference tool for readers interested in tracing imagery through the novel.

Herring, Phillip. *Joyce's Uncertainty Principle.* Princeton, N.J.: Princeton University Press, 1987. Herring distinguishes between what cannot be determined and the authorial "strategy designed to create mystery," uncertainty.

Joyce, Stanislaus. *My Brother's Keeper: James Joyce's Early Years.* Edited with an introduction and notes by Richard Ellmann. Preface by T. S. Eliot. New York: Viking Press, 1958. Intimate view of young Joyce and his concerns from his brother's point of view.

———. *The Dublin Diary of Stanislaus Joyce.* Edited by George Harris Healey. Ithaca, N.Y.: Cornell University Press, 1962. Like *My Brother's Keeper,* useful for Stanislaus's bird's-eye view; the diary moreover is an unrevised view, not written from hindsight.

Kenner, Hugh. *Dublin's Joyce.* Bloomington: Indiana University Press, 1956. Landmark text, especially in the continuing discussion of Joyce's relationship to Stephen.

Levin, Harry. *James Joyce: A Critical Introduction.* Norfolk, Conn.: New Directions, 1941. Rev. ed., 1960. Introduces Joyce and discusses his place in the context of European literature.

MacCabe, Colin. *James Joyce and the Revolution of the Word.* London: Macmillan, 1978. Fascinating poststructural, Lacanian, Marxist reading of Joyce. Particularly helpful in his analysis of how *Portrait* differs from nineteenth-century realistic novels.

Magalaner, Marvin, and Richard M. Kain. *Joyce: The Man, the Work, the Reputation.* New York: New York University Press, 1956. Early, careful discussion of Joyce. Still useful.

Manganiello, Dominic. *Joyce's Politics.* London: Routledge and Kegan Paul, 1980. Concerned with Joyce's responses to Irish nationalism, socialism, fascism; illuminates one of Joyce's cultural contexts.

Morris, William E., and Clifford A. Nault, Jr., eds. *Portraits of an Artist: A Casebook on James Joyce's "A Portrait of the Artist as a Young Man."* New York: Odyssey Press, 1962. Thirty-six previously published com-

Bibliography

mentaries; like Connolly (above) a good collection that reveals the critical views of Joyce's works before 1962.

Noon, William T., S. J. *Joyce and Aquinas.* New Haven, Conn.: Yale University Press, 1957. Best sustained study of Joyce's knowledge and use (or abuse) of Aquinas, both in the aesthetics in *Portrait* and other works.

Riquelme, John Paul. *Teller and Tale in Joyce's Fiction: Oscillating Perspectives.* Baltimore and London: Johns Hopkins University Press, 1983. Fascinating and illuminating poststructuralist consideration of Joyce's narrative techniques.

Scholes, Robert, and Richard M. Kain. *The Workshop of Daedalus: James Joyce and the Raw Material for "A Portrait of the Artist as a Young Man."* Evanston, Ill.: Northwestern University Press, 1965. Crucial collection into one volume of materials, analogues, and versions of *Portrait.* Indispensible for readers interested in Joyce's method.

Staley, Thomas F., and Bernard Benstock, eds. *Approaches to Joyce's "Portrait": Ten Essays.* Pittsburgh: University of Pittsburgh Press, 1976. Ten original essays celebrating the fifty years of *A Portrait.* Contains many excellent studies.

Articles

Beebe, Maurice. "James Joyce: The Return from Exile." In *Ivory Towers and Sacred Founts: The Artist as Hero in Fiction from Goethe to Joyce.* New York: New York University Press, 1964. Seminal essay on Stephen Dedalus's relationship to the tradition of artist/heroes.

Benstock, Bernard. "The Temptation of St. Stephen: A View of the Villanelle." *James Joyce Quarterly* 14 (1976):31–38. Follows Rossman's article (below), focused on Stephen's conception of the villanelle as masturbatory.

Booth, Wayne. "The Problem of Distance in *A Portrait.*" In *The Rhetoric of Fiction.* Chicago: University of Chicago Press, 1961. Argues that the controversy over Joyce's relationship to Stephen stems from a flaw in the novel.

Bowen, Zack. "Stephen's Villanelle: Antecedents, Manifestations, and Aftermath." *Modern British Literature* 5 (1980):63–67. Argues that the villanelle amalgamates Stephen's experiences and rationalizes his self-doubts.

Boyd, Elizabeth. "James Joyce's Hell-Fire Sermons." *Modern Language Notes* 75 (November 1960):11–21.

Carens, James F. "The Motif of Hands in *A Portrait of the Artist as a Young Man.*" *Irish Renaissance Annual* 2 (1981):139–57. Tracing the motif of hands, Carens illuminates the latent homosexuality in the novel as well as making sense of several peculiar passages.

Doherty, James. "Joyce and *Hell Opened to Christians:* The Edition He Used for His 'Hell Sermons.'" *Modern Philology* 61 (November 1963): 109–19.

Feshbach, Sidney. "A Slow and Dark Birth: A Study of the Organization of *A Portrait of the Artist as a Young Man.*" *James Joyce Quarterly* 4 (1967):289–300. Influential study of the novel's structure, focused on images of gestation and birth.

Fortuna, Diana. "The Labyrinth as Controlling Image in Joyce's *Portrait.*" *New York Public Library Bulletin* 76 (1972):120–80. Exhaustive study of labyrinth imagery, arguing Stephen's escape from the labyrinth.

Gabler, Hans Walter. "The Christmas Dinner Scene, Parnell's Death, and the Genesis of *A Portrait of the Artist as a Young Man.*" *James Joyce Quarterly* 13 (1975):27–38. This essay, like Gabler's (in *Approaches,* ed. Staley and Benstock), uses manuscript/typescript evidence to illuminate interpretative cruces in the novel.

Geckle, George L. "Stephen Dedalus and W. B. Yeats: The Making of the Villanelle." *Modern Fiction Studies* 15 (1969):87–96. Argues persuasively Joyce's use of Yeats in the fifth chapter of the novel.

Grayson, Thomas. "James Joyce and Stephen Dedalus: The Theory of Aesthetics." *James Joyce Quarterly* 4 (Summer 1967):310–19. Grayson sees division between Joyce and Stephen, remarking on Stephen's inability to apply his own "stages of apprehension."

Henke, Suzette. "Stephen Dedalus and Woman: A Portrait of the Artist as a Young Misogynist." In *Women in Joyce,* edited by Suzette Henke and Elaine Unkeless. Urbana, Chicago, and London: University of Illinois Press, 1982. For Henke, Stephen's misogyny is his—not Joyce's. Joyce reveals Stephen's immaturity in his treatment of and attitudes about women.

Kenner, Hugh. "Joyce's *Portrait*—a Reconsideration." *University of Windsor Review* 1 (1965):1–15. Kenner modifies his radical, ironic reading of *Portrait,* seeing instead varying distance between Stephen and Joyce.

Naremore, James. "Style as Meaning in *A Portrait of the Artist.*" *James Joyce Quarterly* 4 (Summer 1967):331–42. Studies the changes in style in *Portrait* as a guide to interpretation and characterization; argues that "purple passages" indicate Stephen's immaturity.

Rossman, Charles. "Stephen Dedalus's Villanelle." *James Joyce Quarterly* 12 (1975):281–93. Demonstrates the peculiar nature of Stephen's poem, a fin de siècle production, feeble and derivative. Benstock (above) continues Rossman's argument.

Scholes, Robert. "Stephen Dedalus: Poet or Esthete?" *PMLA* 79 (1964):484–

Bibliography

89. Argues that the villanelle marks Stephen Dedalus's transition from immaturity to maturity and successful artistry.

Sharpless, F. Parvin. "Irony in Joyce's *Portrait:* The Stasis of Pity." *James Joyce Quarterly* 4 (Summer 1967):320–30. Argues that Joyce is both ironic about and sympathetic with his young artist.

Thrane, James R. "Joyce's Sermons on Hell: Its Sources and Its Backgrounds." *Modern Philology* 57 (February 1960):172–98.

Van Ghent, Dorothy. "On *A Portrait of the Artist as a Young Man.*" In *The English Novel: Form and Function.* New York: Rhinehart, 1953. Focuses on the role of language in characterization of Stephen and on his escape from language's labyrinths.

Wilds, Nancy G. "Style and Auctorial Presence in *A Portrait of the Artist as a Young Man.*" *Style* 7 (1973):39–55. Argues that the shifts in style and the ambiguity of relations among reader, writer, and character reveal Joyce.

Bibliographies

Deming, Robert H. *A Bibliography of James Joyce Studies.* 2d ed. Boston: G. K. Hall, 1977.

Rice, Thomas Jackson. *James Joyce: A Guide to Research.* New York and London: Garland Publishing, 1982.

Staley, Thomas F. "James Joyce." In *Anglo-Irish Literature: A Review of Research,* ed. Richard J. Finneran. New York: Modern Language Association, 1976.

INDEX

Anderson, Chester, 117n9
Angeli, Diego (early review), 22, 35
Aquinas, Thomas, 73, 79, 83
Aristotle, 82
Art,
    aestheticism and symbolism, 5–6,
        70–74
    life and, 78, 81
    nationalism and, 71, 105–6
    priesthood and, 70, 77–78, 96–
        97; see also Stephen Dedalus,
        Yeats, and Wilde
    realism and naturalism, 5–6; see
        also Joyce, James and A
        Portrait
    sin and, 71
    See also Stephen Dedalus,
        esthetics

Barth, John, 21
Baudelaire, Charles, 5
Beckett, Samuel, 21
Benstock, Bernard, 120n2
Bettelheim, Bruno: The Uses of
    Enchantment, 38, 39, 40, 43,
    46, 50, 100
Bloom, Harold, 69, 72, 75
Booth, Wayne, 14
Bowen, Zack, 120n2
Bredin, Hughes T., 73
Brivic, Sheldon, 17

Brown, Homer Obed, 16
Budgen, Frank, 107, 109
Byrne, John Francis, 15
Byron, Lord, 73

Chayes, Irene Hendry, 13
Christmas dinner scene. See Portrait
    of the Artist
Clongowes Wood College, 36, 45
Clutton-Brock, A. (early review), 12,
    13
Colum, May and Padriac, 15
Connolly, Thomas, 16
Cope, Jackson I., 67, 68
Cranly (character), 15, 77, 80, 82,
    85–87, 96–97, 101, 105
Curran, Constantine, 15

Daedalus, 23, 63, 65–69, 99, 101,
    102, 103, 119n2
    excavations on Crete, 67, 119n6
    labyrinths and, 62–63, 64, 66, 68
    See also Fatherhood
Davin (character), 29, 77, 78, 81–
    82, 88, 103–4, 105, 106, 107,
    109
Davitt, Michael. See Ireland
Dedalus, Simon (character),
    failures of, 54, 55–57, 59, 61–62,
    63, 65, 75–76

128

Index

ABOUT THE AUTHOR

Marguerite Harkness teaches modern literature and listens to the stories readers tell at Virginia Commonwealth University in Richmond, Virginia. She is the author of *Aesthetics of Dedalus and Bloom* (1984).